D0442193

Commager on Tocqueville

COMMAGER
ON
TOCQUEVILLE

Henry Steele Commager

University of Missouri Press
Columbia and London

Library of Congress Cataloging-in-Publication Data

Commager, Henry Steele, 1902–
    Commager on Tocqueville / Henry Steele Commager.
        p.   cm.
    ISBN 0–8262–0897–5
    1. Tocqueville, Alexis de, 1805–1859—Contributions in
political science. 2. Tocqueville, Alexis de, 1805–1859.
De la démocratie en Amérique. 3. Democracy. 4. Liberty.
5. Justice. 6. Equality.
I. Title.
JC229.T8C63   1993
321.8—dc20   93–2909
                                                     CIP

∞™This paper meets the requirements of the
American National Standard for Permanence of Paper
for Printed Library Materials, Z39.48, 1984.

Designer: Rhonda Miller
Printer and Binder: Thomson-Shore, Inc.
Typeface: Sabon

To Robert H. Ferrell,
friend, colleague, and fellow enthusiast of Tocqueville

CONTENTS

PREFACE

No one who has written about the United States of America was more prescient than Alexis de Tocqueville, the French aristocrat who spent only a few months in this country, whose primary interest was not America at all, but his own France, and whose philosophical concern was not so much democracy as liberty. With an insight that approached genius, Tocqueville saw that the United States held the key to the future, that what America was, Western Europe would inevitably become. His transcendent purpose was therefore to acquaint, to warn, and to prepare France and Europe for the inevitable triumph of equality and for the consequences of that triumph for good and for evil.

Tocqueville's objective, so ardent and so pervasive, so passionate that it was almost an obsession, was quite simply the future of liberty. He hence confronted that problem which has bemused political philosophers since Plato, the reconciliation of liberty and order. This is probably the greatest and most permanent problem in the whole history of government. It was a problem that held captive the attention of Europe's philosophers in the wake of the French Revolution. America in the 1830s was the most democratic of societies; could it help Europeans resolve the questions that pressed upon them as citizens everywhere took up the cry for liberty and equality? Would democratic majorities destroy liberty? Would centralization of power, which democracy made almost inevitable, prove incompatible with liberty? Would individualism—so ruthlessly being exercised on the vast North American continent—be compatible with either democracy or with liberty? And what of justice? There can be no liberty without justice and no justice without order. Can individualism tolerate order? Can democracy be trusted to safeguard justice?

What did Tocqueville envision? When he consulted his hopes he foresaw magnanimity and wisdom guiding the destiny of a Europe yielding to, rather than resisting, the inevitable triumph of democracy, while avoiding or surmounting those shortcomings and flaws that he perceived in the American experiment. When he consulted his fears he recalled that men everywhere prefer equality to liberty, and that if the democratic revolution of the Old World were to be guided by passion, as he suspected it would be in America, the result would be fatal to liberty.

It is a special merit of Tocqueville that he took on the most searching questions about the current and future workings of democracy, and his own primary concern with Europe does not detract in the least from the significance of these questions for Americans. Thus, continued interest in Tocqueville should not surprise us. It is not merely that his work is now recognized as the most profound and most eloquent of all the interpretations of America, nor that what Tocqueville had to say of democracy and equality itself was so profound, nor is it that his deeply religious conservatism appeals to our so-called conservatives today. It is rather that those questions that Tocqueville raised, those warnings that he sounded, those predictions that he so tentatively made, remain more relevant now than in any previous time. In 1887, James Bryce, whose *American Commonwealth* remains the most comprehensive study of America yet made by any foreigner, analyzed the predictions of Tocqueville and found them fascinating but mistaken. Thirty-five years later, in his *Modern Democracies*, Bryce returned to that original position. Would he find Tocqueville's predictions mistaken today? I think not.

The error of Tocqueville, insofar as he can be charged with error, was one of time and of place rather than of foresight or of logic. In a famous but isolated paragraph, he predicted that the future belonged to America and Russia, for though their courses are not the same, he wrote, "each of them seems to be marked out by the will of Heaven to sway the destinies of half the globe." Tocqueville accurately foresaw what we now call the Americanization of the Old World, a process that he read almost entirely in political and social terms. He foresaw it, however, as impending within his own lifetime. The phenomenon was to occur, but not until after World War II, and it appears to be entering a second stage now that the Cold War has stumbled to a close. The remarkable thing about Tocqueville's predictions is not their timeliness, but their ultimate distinction.

Following the Introduction, which places Tocqueville's masterwork, *Democracy in America*, in its proper historical and cultural context, I have chosen five areas to explore, five questions that Tocqueville raised but did not—could not— answer. The questions examined are democracy and the tyranny of the majority, the price of a just society, centralization and democracy, the military in a democracy, and the contradictions between political equality and economic inequality.

As the title of the final chapter suggests, I am not so concerned with what Tocqueville had to say about America and democracy in the 1830s as with what he has to say about democracy and America in the 1990s and after. For what strikes forcibly when reading Tocqueville is the way in which he could make global generalizations on the basis of the American experiment in the 1830s. Are we justified in the 1990s in drawing conclusions on the basis of such generalizations? Yes. With suitable reservations about time, in their extraordinary thoughtfulness they remain as significant, as instructive today as they were a century and a half ago.

And if the present essays, which originated as a series of lectures delivered in 1978, do not appear too hopelessly outdated given the rapidly changing world order of the past fifteen years, it is because of the keen eyes and skilled pens of the scholars and editors who have taken an interest in them. Without their encouragement and expertise, I could never have coerced these lectures into print.

Commager on Tocqueville

INTRODUCTION

For over five centuries the New World has been an object of curiosity to the Old, and for almost half of that time the United States, particularly, has been called upon to point a moral or adorn a tale. Literally thousands of travelers—British, French, and German predominating—have visited here and rushed home to transcribe their impressions: sometimes they have not waited to return but have given a palpitating world their conclusions in advance, as it were. The roll call of British commentators is long and distinguished: it includes, to name only a few of the more prominent, the Trollopes, mother and son, Harriet Martineau, Dickens, Lyell, Grattan, Marryat, Freeman, Spencer, Bryce, and, in our own day, Wells, Bennett, and Chesterton. French visitors and interpreters are less familiar but scarcely less numerous: one bibliography lists some fifteen hundred volumes by French travelers, and the list includes books by Crèvecoeur, Talleyrand, Barbé-Marbois, Chastellux, Chateaubriand, Brissot de Warville, Tocqueville, Considérant, Chevalier, Clemenceau, Jusserand, Tardieu, and Siegfried. No other nation, assuredly, has been subjected to such a literary barrage, exposed to so many million words of praise, blame, and admonition. Only a tough people could have survived.

What is the explanation for this persistent and passionate

curiosity about America, a curiosity whose only parallel in modern history is the contemporary interest in the former Soviet Union? The interest was not fortuitous. Americans are beginning to realize, now, that their country has never been isolated, but Europeans have always known this, for throughout its history America has troubled the Old World. In the sixteenth and seventeenth centuries it was El Dorado, and the nations of Europe fought for the rich prize. In the eighteenth century it became something new under the sun, a republic, a democracy, a federal union, the hope (as Turgot put it) of the human race. Throughout the nineteenth it was a blessing and a menace—and a curiosity. To the poor and oppressed it was the promised land; to the rich and privileged a standing threat; while diplomats everywhere had to reckon with it in their plans and intrigues. Its vast distances and shaggy beauty fired the imagination; its youthful vitality and convulsive growth inspired wonder and respect; its democracy was a challenge, its social equality a rebuke, its toleration a model. If laws of history or of the evolution of society were to be formulated, they must be based in large part upon the American experiment; if new political institutions were to be fashioned, they must be modeled in part upon those of the United States. No statesman could be indifferent to the new nation on the western shores of the Atlantic; no economist could omit it from his calculations; even philosophers and moralists were required to accommodate their speculations to its experience.

Everything about America was astonishing: its broad prairies and majestic rivers; its native peoples, so romantic in prospect, so malevolent in reality; its restless frontier, sweeping across the continent like the tides at St. Michael; the villages that mushroomed overnight into cities; the babel of languages; the blacks who, slave or free, molded society into their own pattern; the farms, large as Old World counties; the democracy of manners so often mistaken for vulgarity; the spectacle of Catholics and Protestants living amicably side by side, and of scores and hundreds of other sects; the singular notion of free public education and the confusion of schools and colleges; the disconcerting freedom of women and the purity of morals; the town meeting, the state legislature, the political party, the popular election of a chief magistrate; the disparity of wealth and the blurring of class distinctions; the fabulous prosperity, the buoyant confidence, the latent power. No wonder it took a thousand essays to penetrate to the truth about America.

Americans themselves gave little help. Notwithstanding that nervous boastfulness which impressed so many visitors, Americans, on the whole, gave but a poor account of themselves—certainly a confusing one. Their newspapers played up the sensational and the eccentric; their literature reflected an unfamiliar local color or, more recently, mirrored a society incredibly violent and rude; their politicians indulged in antics that seemed, and often were, preposterous; and that somehow the political machine worked smoothly enough seemed rather a dispensation of Providence than a tribute to common sense. In our own day, the moving picture, easily the most influential of interpreters, gave a fabulous picture of wealth, crime, vulgarity, speed, excitement, salacity, and abnormality. In Britain nature seemed to conform to art, and from the days of Fielding and Smollett to those of Wells and Bennett, the library was a not unsatisfactory substitute for travel, but it was inconceivable that America could be what, on her many surfaces, she appeared to be. The picture was diverse and contradictory, and the least discerning foreigner could confidently predict that America would be unpredictable.

It must be admitted that European visitors did little to resolve the confusion. Most of the literature of description and interpretation, English as well as continental, is pretty shoddy stuff. The interpretation of national character is difficult enough in the most auspicious of circumstances: the circumstances attending the writings of European visitors were rarely auspicious. Of all the thousands of books on America, perhaps less than two score are of lasting value.

Why is the average so low, why are so many of the accounts mediocre or worse? Why, especially, have men and women otherwise thoughtful, learned, and observant, failed so signally to understand and interpret the United States? The question is not relevant to the works of a Grattan, a Münsterberg, or a Bryce, but it is properly directed to the overwhelming majority of the commentators, British and continental. Only a partial explanation can be submitted here. Many, if not most, of those who wrote about America, came here with a closed mind, came not to learn but to confirm preconceived notions. They assumed—naturally enough—that the Old World was the norm and interpreted every deviation from that norm as quaint, vulgar, or eccentric. That Americans, who had inherited admirable political, legal, religious, and social institutions, preferred to fashion new ones appeared to them faintly perverse. Few of those who wrote so glibly on America saw the whole of it, or saw any part of it thoroughly: altogether too many got their impressions of the American countryside from the windows of a train, their impressions of cities from hotel lobbies or dining rooms. Others, overwhelmed with the vastness and variety of American life, took refuge in anecdotes or in exclamatory descriptions of the picturesque and the exceptional. Some visitors were inspired by purely business considerations—the search for land, for business openings, for investment opportunities. Still others, with their eye on royalties, made a book the excuse for their visit rather than the visit the justification for their book; what they wrote, therefore, was designed to titillate or flatter a British or European audience—an audience notoriously uncritical and credulous in everything concerning America. Finally, of all those who attempted to interpret America, only a handful were intellectually competent to the task: of most of them it could be said, as the sage Franklin said in another connection, "their poor noddles were distracted."

These observations apply with less force, perhaps, to French than to British visitors and commentators. The French had, to be sure, a clearer field, an easier task. There was no tradition of enmity to embarrass relations between Americans and French, but one of friendship: Lafayette proved as immortal as George III. From America, France had neither so much to fear nor so much to hope as Britain. Its relation was avuncular rather than maternal, and it could regard the new nation with an objectivity scarcely possible to the mother country. Then, too, France had had her revolution, and she needed neither to borrow nor to resist American radicalism; nor was America draining France of her population, nor threatening her supremacy in commerce, manufacturing, or business. Nor were the two peoples divided—to adapt Shaw's hackneyed phrase—by the barrier of a common language and common institutions. The British were inclined to regard any departure from English ways as a reflection upon themselves and, at the same time, to resent imitations as the possessors of the genuine commonly resent those who urge the merits of the counterfeit: the French, who were not looking for a New France, were not outraged when they failed to find a New Britain.

To most of these melancholy generalizations, as well as to

their Gallic qualifications, Alexis de Tocqueville is an exception. He was thorough and indefatigable in his search for facts, patient and skillful in their organization, sympathetic and perspicacious in their interpretation, luminous in their presentation. His purpose was lofty, his learning solid, his understanding profound. By common consent his *Democracy in America* is the most illuminating commentary on American character and institutions ever penned by a foreigner, the one which, a century after its appearance, seems best assured of immortality.

"I confess that in America, I saw more than America; I sought the image of democracy itself, with its inclinations, its character, its prejudices, and its passions, in order to learn what we have to fear or to hope from its progress." So wrote Tocqueville, and the confession is basic to an understanding of his work. When we reflect that Tocqueville never returned to the United States, that he did not keep up with his American friends and associates, or retain any serious interest in the course of American affairs, or take note in subsequent editions of his great books of those changes that were transforming American society and which called into question the validity of some of his generalizations and challenged some of his predictions, we may assume that he lacked any serious interest in the United States, except the interest that the scientist has in the laboratory. America was, it seemed, merely that laboratory. The primary object of his investigation was not the country itself, but rather democracy—a word that Tocqueville used much as we use it today to embrace social and economic as well as political practices and institutions. The inspiration of the inquiry was not so much curiosity about America as concern for France especially, and for the Old World in general; the findings were designed for application abroad.

For democracy, Tocqueville was persuaded, was inevitable and irresistible, its doctrines and practices destined to spread over the Western world. The invasion of England was already under way: Tocqueville's brief visit there had persuaded him of that, and every letter from J. S. Mill or from Nassau Senior strengthened the persuasion. France could not escape, France whose tradition of liberty and equality made her peculiarly susceptible; before long the ferment of democracy would be at work in all the nations of Europe. "The question here discussed," wrote Tocqueville, "is interesting not only to the United States, but to the whole world; it concerns not a nation, but all mankind."

Yet if democracy was inevitable, would not mere description suffice? Here we come to the heart of Tocqueville's thought. Democracy was, indeed, inevitable, but democracy was no simple thing but infinitely complex, not a rigid system or an implacable doctrine but an attitude of mind and a habit of conduct. It was a mixture of good and evil—Tocqueville was not always sure which was predominant—but it was possible to separate the good from the evil. It was possible, above all, to separate the natural from the artificial, the universal from the particular, to accommodate democracy to its various environments.

Tocqueville was one of the first students of politics to discern the truth—so often ignored or condemned in our own day—that the great forces of history do not operate uniformly and automatically in every society, but are naturalized, as it were, wherever they appear. He proposed, for France, a reconciliation of fatalism and free will, of the iron forces of history and the genius of the nation. "The more I study the former state of the world," he wrote,

> and indeed even when I see the modern world in greater detail,
> when I consider the prodigious diversity found there, not just
> in the laws but in the principles of the laws, and the different
> forms that the right of property has taken . . . I am tempted to
> the belief that what are called necessary institutions are only
> institutions to which one is accustomed, and that in matters of
> social constitution the field of possibilities is much wider than
> people living within each society imagine.

The field of possibilities was more extensive than men
imagined! Here was the real justification for the study of
democracy in America. Democracy was on the march, but
the manner in which it was to come, the form it was to take,
the consequences it was to have, were all matters over which
men might exercise control. For everything that concerned
democracy, America was not only the most convenient but
also the most elaborate laboratory. It held the answers to the
questions that were bound to trouble the Old World. Can
men govern themselves? Is it possible to reconcile liberty and
order, the individual and the state? Does democracy but
substitute the tyranny of the majority for the tyranny of the
few? Can any government tolerate free speech and a free
press, or will liberty inevitably degenerate into license? Can
men of different races, tongues, and faiths live amicably side
by side? Will the melting pot, with its fusing of peoples,
produce an inferior race? Will universal education be accom-
panied by a vulgarization of culture? Can art, literature, and
philosophy flourish in a society that substitutes the verdict of
the majority for the judgment of training and tradition? Is
democracy synonymous with mediocrity, and is the well-
being of the many worth the sacrifice of beauty and grace?
Will democracy so depreciate the military virtues as to

expose itself to enervation from within and destruction from without?

No scholar could hope to find conclusive answers to questions so profound and so complex, but that the American experience might illuminate the problem was apparent, for America was the proving ground of history. Here, as James Russell Lowell was shortly to observe, the elements are all in solution, and we have only to look to see how they will combine. "History, which every day makes less account of governors and more of man, must find here the compendious key to all that picture writing of the Past."

It was, to be sure, the key to the future rather than to the past that Tocqueville sought, but that America held the key to this, too, was clear. It was clear, at least, to young Tocqueville—who was the first to appreciate the scientific possibilities of the New World—and *Democracy in America* vindicated his judgment and his vision.

It is just over one hundred and fifty years, now, since young Tocqueville—he was barely thirty—brought out the first two volumes of *Democracy in America*. He was filled with misgivings—and so was his publisher, M. Gosselin. But soon the book was acclaimed on two continents and crowned by the French Academy, and M. Gosselin was delighted. "So it appears that your book is a masterpiece," he boasted, rubbing his hands together. It was the comment of a tradesman, said Tocqueville with a sneer. But it was, too, the verdict of posterity.

What explains the fame, the longevity, of *Democracy in America*? No other book of its kind has weathered so well, none has been so frequently reprinted, and without misgivings even by publishers.

The book, certainly, is not without faults. It is, for all its sharpness and spareness, overlong—two more volumes appeared in 1840, making four in all. It makes no concessions to the reader, either in analysis or in interpretation; it has no narrative quality; it is devoid of humor. It includes much that is merely descriptive; it omits much that is important.

To draw up a general indictment and itemize a bill of particulars is, indeed, no difficult task. Tocqueville came not to observe America as a whole, but to observe the operations of democracy, and democracy, rather than America, it must never be forgotten, was his primary concern. He tended to substitute his own reflections for facts, or, where the facts were stubborn, to force them into his own preconceived pattern. When he wrote the second—and best—part of *Democracy in America*, the sharp impact of personal experience was fading, the pressure of France was strong, and Tocqueville indulged himself more readily in rationalization, yielded increasingly to the temptations of a priori reasoning. He did not sufficiently check what he felt was bound to happen with what actually was happening, and where history ran counter to his predictions he was inclined to give the impression that history was somehow at fault. Thus he could write at length, and ominously, of the tyranny of the majority without once citing a convincing example of such tyranny. His acquaintance with America was limited; he knew the East better than the West, the North better than the South. His investigations were haphazard rather than systematic, his sources of information inadequate and often misleading. He made it a point to meet the best people, and the best people, then as now, were inclined to deprecate democracy: Justice Story complained, with reason, that Tocqueville had borrowed liberally from his commentaries, and Story was a high Federalist. An aristocrat, Tocqueville exaggerated the importance of manners, and he was capable of the observation that nothing is more prejudicial to democracy than its outward forms of behavior, that many men would willingly endure its vices who cannot support its manners. He was not sufficiently familiar with the English background of American institutions, and he frequently mistook for peculiarly American or peculiarly democratic what was merely Anglo-American. He missed many things that less perceptive observers saw, possibly because the obvious did not always accommodate itself to his philosophical pattern; in his anxiety to get below the surface he failed to appreciate things that were on the surface. Thus he could argue the ultimate disintegration of the Union because he failed to notice economic developments or to comprehend the nationalizing effect of the industrial revolution. He missed the abolition movement, and transcendentalism, and his interest in penal and prison reform—the ostensible ground for his visit to America—did not persuade him to study the reform movement in general. For all his concern with democracy, he seemed singularly uninterested in its immediate political manifestations, and the casual reader of his book would scarcely realize that while Tocqueville was traversing America, Andrew Jackson was president.

These are serious defects, defects that would guarantee oblivion to most volumes of description or interpretation. Yet *Democracy in America* has not only survived oblivion; it has earned for itself a place as a classic. For the faults of the book are, after all, superficial rather than fundamental; they are grievous only with reference to the standards that Tocqueville himself set, and those standards were incomparably high. The omissions, the inadequacies, the misconceptions of the book can easily be supplied or corrected by other books.

And what are the merits of *Democracy in America*? First, it can be said, Tocqueville chose a great and noble theme and handled it with dignity. That theme was the adjustment of the civilizations of Western Christendom to democracy. Others had written about America; Tocqueville undertook to relate American to world history, to fix the significance of America in history. His subject, he wrote in all humility, is interesting to the whole world; it concerns, not a nation, but all mankind. His purpose was to prepare men everywhere for the "providential fact" of equality; to dissipate fears, quiet excessive hopes, encourage accommodation; to lift men above narrow and selfish and persuade them to broad and generous views. There is almost a Periclean quality about his own statement of his grand design:

> I have sought to show what a democratic people is in our days, and by this delineation, executed with rigorous accuracy, my design has been to produce a twofold effect on my contemporaries. To those who make to themselves an ideal democracy, a brilliant vision which they think it easy to realize, I undertake to show that they have arrayed their future in false colours; that the democratic government they advocate, if it be of real advantage to those who can support it, has not the lofty features they ascribe to it; and moreover, that this government can only be maintained on certain conditions of intelligence, private morality, and religious faith, which we do not possess; and that its political results are not to be obtained without labour.
>
> To those for whom the word "democracy" is synonymous with disturbance, anarchy, spoliation, and murder, I have attempted to show that the government of democracy may be reconciled with respect for property, with deference for rights, with safety to freedom, with reverence to religion; that if

democratic government is less favorable than another to some of the finer parts of human nature, it has also great and noble elements; and that perhaps, after all, it is the will of God to shed a lesser grade of happiness on the totality of mankind, not to combine a greater share of it on a smaller number, or to raise the few to the verge of perfection. I have undertaken to demonstrate to them that, whatever their opinion on this point may be, it is too late to deliberate, that society is advancing and dragging them along with itself towards equality of conditions; that the sole remaining alternative lies between evils henceforth inevitable; that the question is not whether aristocracy or democracy can be maintained, but whether we are to live under a democratic society, devoid indeed of poetry and greatness, but at least orderly, moral, or under a democratic society, lawless and depraved, abandoned to the frenzy of revolution or subjected to a yoke heavier than any of those which have crushed mankind since the fall of the Roman Empire. I have sought to calm the ardour of the former class of persons, and, without discouragement, to point out the only path before them. I have sought to allay the terrors of the latter, and to bend their minds to the idea of an inevitable future, so that with less impetuosity on the one hand, and less resistance on the other, the world may advance more peaceably to the necessary fulfilment of its destiny. This is the fundamental idea of the book; an idea which connects all its other ideas in a single web.

And to his friend Kergolat, he confessed, "To labour in this direction is in my eyes a *sainte occupation,* and one in which one must spare neither one's money nor one's time, nor one's life."

Tocqueville chose a great subject, and he measured up to its greatness. He was the first philosophical historian to write of the American experiment; the first political scientist to make democracy the primary object of realistic investigation. It must be accounted a capital merit in Tocqueville that he had not only a philosophy, but also the right philosophy.

He saw that the significance of America in history was to be found in the opportunity that it afforded as a laboratory of social, economic, and political democracy, and he fastened his attention on that aspect of America to the exclusion of the merely picturesque or sensational. He had an instinct for the jugular vein in history.

Other observers had lost themselves in the trivial, the irrelevant, the inconsequential; they maundered on about hotel service, the litter on the streets of cities, the hardships of railroad travel, the table manners of their hosts. Tocqueville, too, noted these things, but he did not suppose they were important in themselves or permit them to distract his attention from the object of his investigation—the effect of democracy on manners and morals, politics and religion, business and labor, literature and art, family and social relations. He was concerned, throughout, with fundamental causes and ultimate consequences.

On almost every page of his book we discern the play of an alert, inquisitive, and critical mind. It is a tribute to the triumph of Tocqueville's method that we are, throughout, more interested in what he has to say about a subject than we are in the subject itself. He had, that is, not only a philosophical but an eminently reflective mind; he had not only a philosophy of history, in the grand manner, but perspicacity and penetration; he was as illuminating in his particular as in his general observations. We are constantly gratified by his shrewd insights and his happy prophecies. Who, after all, has better comprehended the American character than this French stranger who arrived at his understanding almost as by a mathematical formula, so rigorous was his analysis, so logical his conclusions? In his day our literature was still strongly colonial, but Tocqueville foresaw with astonishing insight the effect that democracy would have upon it in the future. He saw, too, that democracy must have its own history, one in which the individual was subordinate to the mass, fortuity to great sweeping movements; and from George Bancroft to Henry Adams and Charles Beard, American historical literature has conformed to Tocqueville's formula. He penetrated to the gnawing uncertainty of many Americans about social democracy, the pretentiousness and insincerity of much of the talk about the common man by men who invariably made it clear that they themselves were uncommon men. He understood, as have few foreigners and not many Americans, the combination—peculiarly prominent in the realm of politics—of extravagance of language and prudence of conduct. He noted, as had others, the American passion for change, and he found it the natural consequence of the restless search for the ideal and the opportunities afforded all Americans to achieve that ideal. He grasped the fact, as yet concealed from many of our agitated Bourbons, that democracy makes for conservatism and that the surest guarantee of stability is the wide distribution of property. He was the first foreign observer to appreciate the significance of the dominance of the American political scene by men trained to the law, and he described in terms still relevant that aristocracy of the robe which Americans take for granted but which other democratic peoples look upon with astonishment. He saw the significance of the interaction of democracy and religion and emphasized throughout his study the place of the church in American life. He discerned the natural hostility to the military in a democracy, but he foresaw with startling accuracy the effect of prolonged war on American society and economy and psychology. There was little, indeed, in the American character that his penetrating eye did not see, his luminous mind comprehend.

Tocqueville's interpretation, for all his aristocratic and alien background, was almost unfailingly judicious. He was misled, at times, by the men he consulted, the books he read, but his errors were never malicious. His view of democracy was often pessimistic, but never jaundiced, and it is gratifying that America has confounded its most astute critic where he was pessimistic rather than where he was optimistic. No other interpreter of America, not Grattan nor Bryce, not Münsterberg nor Brogan, has achieved the aloofness, the objectivity, the serene impersonality, that came naturally to Tocqueville. The explanation is, largely, in Tocqueville's own character; it is, in part, that Tocqueville was concerned to instruct his own people rather than to edify the Americans, and that patriotism and morality inexorably required the most scrupulous objectivity.

Finally, it must be counted among the great merits of *Democracy in America* that its style is felicitous and even brilliant. There are no purple patches, there are few epigrams, but there is, throughout, a brilliant clarity, a resiliency, a toughness, that contrasts sharply with the rhetoric of Trollope or Martineau, the verbosity of Bryce, the strained brilliance of Siegfried or Maurois. Tocqueville has, above all others who have written about America, the magisterial style.

It is this happy combination of a great theme with a philosophy profound enough to comprehend it, a temperament judicious enough to interpret it, an intelligence acute enough to master it, a style adequate to its demands, that makes *Democracy in America* one of the great and enduring works of political literature. As a young man Tocqueville confessed that he did not know any way of life more honorable or more attractive than to write with such honesty about the great truths that one's name became known to the civilized world. It is a safe prophecy that as long as democracy itself endures, Tocqueville's name will be known to the civilized world.

ONE

Democracy and the Tyranny of the Majority

Democracy, as it was being defined in nineteenth-century America and debated in Europe, had given a new dimension to the ancient problem of liberty. It presented on the one hand the promise of a larger, more encompassing, and more benevolent freedom, and on the other the threat of a new kind of tyranny, one for which the societies of the Old World were unprepared. For what now remains of those barriers that formerly arrested tyranny, Tocqueville asked, since religion has lost its empire over the souls of men, the most prominent boundary that divides good from evil is overthrown, and everything seems doubtful and indeterminate in the moral world? Kings and nations are guided by chance, and none can say where are the natural limits of despotism. Revolutions have forever destroyed the respect that surrounds rulers of the state, and since they have been relieved from the burden of public esteem, princes may henceforth surrender themselves without fear to the intoxication of arbitrary power. (For princes, you can of course read führers or other leaders who took over in the twentieth century.)

Let us begin, then, with what is indubitably the most familiar and perhaps the most influential of Tocqueville's prognostications, that because in a democracy the majority will inevitably seek to tyrannize over minorities, democracy may prove incompatible with liberty. It was not a new idea, not even in America, nor is it one that has outlived its use; I do not say its usefulness. It was the very basis of the argument for checks and balances that John Adams elaborated in his ponderous defense of the constitutions of the United States. It runs like a black thread through the arguments of the state ratifying conventions of the 1780s by those whom Cecelia Kenyon has called "men of little faith." It was sound Federalist doctrine in Hamilton, Fisher Ames, and Gouverneur Morris, even though less ostentatiously in Justice John Marshall, and it was accepted by his ablest contemporary, Chancellor Kent of New York. The argument is almost too familiar to reiterate. A few samples will suffice.

Here is John Adams, who elaborated the theory more than any other, reminding his countrymen that "the experience of all ages has proved that the people constantly give away their liberties. The management of the executive and judicial powers together always corrupts them, and throws the whole power into the hands of the most profligate and abandoned among them." And he added that if the majority were ever to control the government, "debts would be abolished, taxes laid heavy on the rich and not at all on others, and the idle, the vicious, the intemperate would rush into the utmost extravagance of debauchery."

Here is Alexander Hamilton in his dramatic attack on the Virginia and New Jersey Plans of Union: "The voice of the people has been said to be the voice of God, however, generally this maxim has been outdated. It is not true to fact. Give therefore to the rich a distinct and permanent share of the government. They will check the unsteadiness of the second branch whose turbulence and uncontrollable disposition requires checks."

Or to paraphrase Chancellor Kent, resisting to the end the proposal to draw from the suffrage in New York State: "The extreme democratic principle when applied to the legislative and executive departments has been regarded with terror by the wise men of every age because in every European republic, ancient or modern, in which it has been tried, it has terminated disastrously, and been productive of corruption in justice, violence, and tyranny. Dare we flatter ourselves that we are a peculiar people, a question that has run down the corridors of our history and been answered by a resounding yes from one side and a querulous no from the other."

Fear of equality has always been with us, and fear of democracy too, and we could compile a depressing anthology of jeremiads from the early years of the Republic to the collapse of the southern Confederacy. To do so, however, would be an exercise in masochism. Captiousness of human depravity was, of course, deeply rooted in Puritanism, where it was, intellectually at least, respectable. It lingered on, long after its religious rationale had been dissipated, to find dubious justifications and misgivings about the impact of social equality upon a stable and comfortable society, a society that feared any undermining, any subversion of its prosperity, feared also political equality and the civility of the legal order, as well as the degeneration of Puritan morality into private irritability.

When we contemplate the objections that emerged in the early years of the Republic, we must agree with Henry Adams in that famous paragraph where he writes that the obstinacy of the race was never better shown than when, with the sunlight of the nineteenth century burst in upon them, those resolute sons of granite and ice turned their faces from the sight and smiled in their sardonic way at the folly and wickedness of men who would pretend to believe that the world improved because henceforth the ignorant and the vicious were to rule the United States and govern the churches and schools of New England.

In one form or another, this debate, launched at the very birth of the Republic, still persists; the debate between those who believe that government is safe only in the hands of those whom John Adams called the rich and the wellborn and the able, and those who ask rather the question Jefferson put in his first inaugural address: "Sometimes it is said that man cannot be trusted with the government of himself. Can he, then, be trusted with the government of others? Or have we found angels in the forms of kings to govern him?"

The persistence of this controversy is not surprising, for it centers on a paradox inherent in the philosophy and structure of our government and perhaps never is to be resolved. It is a paradox that has perplexed our wisest statesmen. Here is Jefferson, putting it almost unconsciously in that same first inaugural address: "All," he said, "will bear in mind this sacred principle, that though the will of the majority is in all cases to prevail, that will, to be rightful, must be reasonable." Sixty years later, Lincoln, himself a minority president, asserted that a majority held in restraint by constitutional checks and limitations is the only true sovereign of a free people. Whoever rejects it does of necessity fly into anarchy or despotism.

There it is. All power inheres in the people, but the people may not exercise all power. The will of the majority must prevail, but only if it is righteous. The majority is a true sovereign, but only when held in check by balances and limitations. It is a dualism that might be expected to baffle, if not paralyze, a people less resourceful than the Americans. They not only took it in their stride but triumphantly institutionalized it in their constitutional structure, for as the American Constitution was the first in history to incorporate the principle that men make government and that all government derives its authority from consent, it was also the first to place effective limits on government.

No wonder Tocqueville was baffled. He saw that in America the people were sovereign and had all power, and he knew that all power corrupts. He was familiar with the complex system of checks and limits that Americans had constructed to restrain the misuse of power and acknowledged that these were effective. But he knew, too, that the temptations of tyranny were stronger than the attractions of self-restraint, and he suspected that they were irresistible and predicted therefore a new kind of tyranny, one that would operate within the framework of constitutionalism but would nevertheless be just as inimical to liberty as the older and more familiar forms of tyranny that had crushed liberty through the whole of history. He predicted the tyranny of opinion.

Listen to him as he designs variations on this argument: first the indictment, as it were, next the specification of the error, and finally the sober prediction of consequences. In the principle of equality he very clearly discerned two tendencies, one leading the mind of every man to untried thoughts, the other prohibiting him from thinking at all. Under the dominion of certain laws, democracy would extinguish that liberty of the mind in which the democratic social condition is favorable, so that after having broken all the bondage once imposed upon it by ranks or by men, the human mind would be closely fettered to the general will by the greatest number.

Along with this is a series of almost aphoristic accusations: "The power of the majority in America," he said, is "not only preponderant, but irresistible"; "No obstacles exist which can impede or so much as retard its progress, or which can induce it to heed the complaints of those whom it crushes upon its path"; "the power of the majority surpasses all the powers with which we are acquainted in Europe." These are disparate, unconnected observations, but they all say the same thing. "Freedom of opinion does not exist in America." "So long as a majority is still undecided, discussion is carried on; but as soon as its decision is irrevocably pronounced, a submissive silence is observed; and the friends, as well as the opponents of a measure, unite in assenting to its propriety."

What all this means is that in America, legislature is supreme, so said Tocqueville. It is under a legal despotism, it is indeed a legal despotism, and this favors too the arbitrary power of the magistrate. The majority, he concluded, therefore has absolute power both to make laws and to watch over their execution. The result is indeed sobering:

> I know of no country in which there is so little true independence of mind and freedom of discussion as in America. . . . The sovereign can no longer say, "You shall think as I do on pain of death"; but he says, "You are free to think differently from me, and to retain your life, your property, and all you possess; but if such be your determination, you are henceforth an alien among your people. You may retain your civil rights, but they will be useless to you. . . . You will remain among men, but you will be deprived of the rights of mankind. Your fellow-creatures will shun you like an impure being; and those who are most persuaded of your innocence will abandon you too, lest they should be shunned in turn."

This also proved a somber prediction of what happened in the McCarthy era.

Following that conclusion came the ominous forecast: "If ever the free institutions of America are destroyed, that event may be attributed to the unlimited authority of the majority, which may at some future time urge minorities to desperation, and oblige them to have recourse to physical force.

Anarchy will then be the result, but it will have been brought about by despotism."

That Tocqueville's argument, based as it was wholly upon deductive reasoning, his logic flawed and his facts erroneous, has nevertheless commanded respect down to our own day is a tribute to his genius for intuitive insights. For though Tocqueville does not submit a scintilla of evidence drawn from the America of his own day to support these allegations of majority tyranny, we are uncomfortably aware that the future was to provide evidence enough, evidence to give comfort to the enemies of democracy. Although majority tyranny triumphed only briefly and sporadically in the United States (outside of the South), we know that it did in other modern democracies, with consequences more tragic than even Tocqueville could have imagined, as he was concerned with democracy in Europe rather than the United States.

Let us follow Tocqueville as he deals with the American scene and in American terms. Here we stumble at the very threshold at his almost willful failure to define his terms *tyranny* and *majority*. As we have known it, tyranny is arbitrary power, oppression, despotism, the authority of the gallows and the faggot and the rack. What Tocqueville had in mind was not this tyranny, not the tyranny of St. Bartholomew's Eve or the revocation of the Edict of Nantes, of James II and Lord Chief Justice Jeffries, of Robespierre, who had sent Tocqueville's grandfather to the guillotine, or of Napoleon. Nor was it the tyranny that drove Roger Williams to Narragansett Bay or smothered Quakers to death in the Bay Colony, or even that lawless violence which Patriots visited upon hapless Loyalists. No, it was something new, something peculiar to democracy, the tyranny of public opinion. It was moral, it was intellectual, it was psychological. It was disapproval of, and hostility and ostracism toward, those who would not conform, and it affected chiefly those whose convictions were superficial or whose courage was weak or whose positions were vulnerable. Doubtless such a tyranny was pernicious, but it was after all less dangerous than the more overt tyrannies of the Old World.

What of the term *majority?* The United States of the 1830s was the one nation where the concept of majority was respectable, the one nation where it was most nearly realized in practice in the Western world. Yet not during Tocqueville's lifetime, not perhaps until our own time, has it been fairly tested. While suffrage was broader in the United States in Tocqueville's day than elsewhere on the globe, it still did not represent a majority of the population. Not remotely, for it was limited to white adult males who met whatever qualifications state constitutions might impose upon its exercise. Blacks who were slave or free were everywhere excluded from the suffrage. So were women, and of course, those under twenty-one. Of those who were entitled to vote, somewhat less than one-fourth of the population, only a minority, generally bothered to exercise the right, except in presidential elections and a few hotly contested local elections. Approximately forty percent of those entitled to vote actually did so in the election of 1832, somewhat over fifty percent in 1840, and as much as sixty percent in 1852, which is about where we have got now. This was spectacular by Old World standards, but it still did not constitute a majority, only a majority of a minority, and it furnished therefore a most dubious basis for generalizations about majority tyranny.

Had Tocqueville chosen to pursue this thesis of majority tyranny later in life, that is, in his own life, he might have made out almost an incontrovertible case in his own country. In December 1851, over 8 million Frenchmen representing an overwhelming majority of the adult males went to the polls and ratified Louis Napoleon's coup d'état by a vote of 7.5 million in favor and 650,000 against. It was a dusky vindication.

But if we look to our own history, as Tocqueville did not when he formulated his history of majority tyranny, we find only sporadic and local examples of anything approaching majority tyranny, whether in the realm of politics or even in the realm of opinion. It is easy enough to recount these, and if we were to string together every example of tyranny from the Alien and Sedition Acts to Lincoln's wartime infringements on the freedom of the press, from the Ku Klux Klan in the Reconstruction era to McCarthyism in the 1950s, the chain would be formidable. But we should keep in mind Jefferson's response to the hysterical fears excited by Shays's Rebellion, that one rebellion in thirteen states in the course of eleven years—he might have said in the course of a hundred—is but one in a century and a half. No country should be so long without one.

Perhaps the most interesting observation to make of the Alien and Sedition Acts is, after all, that they inspired the Kentucky and Virginia Resolutions and were wiped off the statute books within two years. There was tyranny of a sort early in the nineteenth century in Rhode Island, but it was tyranny of a minority over a majority, and tyranny that skulked behind an archaic constitution, namely, the original charter. It was a majority that agitated and almost fought for the right of manhood suffrage, and won it, too—I speak of course of Dorr's so-called Rebellion. It was tyranny, just the kind Tocqueville had in mind, in the persecution of the Mormons both in Illinois and in Missouri. But the Mormons found refuge in the West, set up their own commonwealth, and proceeded to establish a majoritarian rule of their own, which a good many gentiles regarded as tyranny.

Clearly, the major example of tyranny in America, and we have only one clear-cut example of tyranny by definition, is slavery. Let us observe, however, several interesting things there: first that, oddly enough, though Tocqueville devoted a chapter to slavery and races in the United States, he did not cite slavery as an example of tyranny in his general discussion of that subject. This was, as it turned out, rather wise, because what we had here was quite clearly a tyranny of a minority, not a majority, a minority of slaveholders among southerners and the minority of all the whites in the nation itself. We need not enter into anything as familiar as that. Where, as I recall, the number of slaveholders in the United States in 1860 was 352,000, the white population of the South, the slaveholding South, was perhaps 8 million. The total number of the slaveholders in the South themselves represented a distinct minority, which alone was committed to slavery; though that South did extend to Delaware and Maryland, it was certainly a minority section of the United States.

In another sense, perpetuation of white supremacy even after the legal end of slavery did vindicate Tocqueville's insight. For just as nonslaveholders in the South supported slavery and were prepared to fight for it to the bitter end at Appomattox, and to nullify emancipation or at least to nullify freedom afterward, so the majority of whites both North and South perpetuated the principle of white supremacy all through the nineteenth and well into the twentieth century.

Slavery is gone. Constitutionally, blacks are entitled to all the rights and privileges of others and to equal protection of the laws. Yet discrimination lingers on. This can probably not be labeled tyranny, but doubtless to its victims it seems much like that.

While Tocqueville saw no solution to the problem of slavery and predicted that it would eventually destroy the Union, and perhaps democracy as well, he was aware of those countervailing forces that might mitigate majority tyranny among Americans. Americans, he pointed out, had made great and successful efforts to counteract the imperfections of human nature and to correct the natural defects of democracy, and he referred to the township system in New England; the strength of local attachments everywhere; the closeness of representatives to those who chose them; the factors of annual or frequent elections, which foreshadowed the later referendum; the role of political parties, which drew their juices from the people; the shifting tides of party strength; and the experience of the people themselves in self-government. His conclusion was a tribute to the patent good sense, indeed the political genius, of the American people: "To evils which are common to all democratic peoples, they have applied remedies which none but themselves had ever thought of before, and although they were the first to make the experiment, they have succeeded in it. The manners and laws of Americans are not the only ones which may suit a democratic people; but the Americans have shown that it would be wrong to despair of regulating democracy by the aid of manners and of laws."

Tocqueville is prepared to recognize this, but not to build upon it. Perhaps nowhere else in his *Democracy in America* does he so stubbornly reject reality for speculation. In this, almost needless to say, he has had many and more reckless successors.

For in fact nothing was more impressive about American

democracy than the passion and the ingenuity with which Americans had celebrated their newfound freedom by devising elaborate restraints upon it and upon government, the most elaborate restraints, indeed, known to history. The contrast here between the American and the French revolutions was dramatic and sobering. Written constitutions in America, state and national, separations of powers, bills of rights that protected not only procedural but substantive liberties, the supremacy of civil power over the military power, bicameral legislatures, intricate checks and balances within every governmental structure, a federal system that distributed authority among government, judicial review of legislative acts and of executive conduct, political parties and a two-party system that imposed compromise on all its members and elements, recurrence at frequent and exact intervals to the popular will, power to impeach or remove offending public servants: all these were some of the formal checks that were designed by Americans to make official tyranny almost impossible.

Alongside these, Americans developed and still retain informal limits on power, probably no less effective than the formal. There is the elementary fact of size, which, especially in the early years of the Republic, favored legal and religious diversity, and which implacably imposed upon the American people the habit of concession and compromise. The one time that failed, namely in 1860, the Union broke asunder. There was a safety valve of mobility, geographical mobility on a continental scale, social and economic mobility within the national social scale, which effectively discouraged the development anywhere of a class order. There was—Tocqueville was one of the first to perceive this—that habit of voluntary association, to which we shall return, which constantly and ubiquitously created new interest groups, new alignments, new counterbalancing elements in society. There was the principle of the open door for immigration, which introduced, indeed invited into the body politic, ever new and unknown elements, whose impact could not be foreseen by or regulated by government. And along with all this was a negative factor of immense significance, the absence in the New World of those deep and passionate attachments or commitments, religious, ideological, or class, which elsewhere nourished and presided over fanaticism.

Americans, almost alone of Western people, have never had genuine religious wars, or even religious persecution, nothing like the persecution of the Huguenots, nothing like the pogroms against the Jews in Russia and elsewhere. The American parties are not ideological but mostly innocent of ideas, and their objectives are not to change society but to change office, a very legitimate objective, by the way, perhaps much better than the objective of changing society.

We can indeed put the matter more positively. The record of that half century of democracy which Tocqueville was able to observe up to the Jacksonian era demonstrated that majorities, that is, majorities of the existing body politic, far from being instruments of tyranny, had everywhere, except in the South where slavery was the issue, supported and advanced the causes of democracy and of freedom. They have written and endorsed the state constitutions and insisted upon adding bills of rights eventually to all of them, and when the Federal Constitution appeared without such a bill of rights, it was public opinion, skillfully organized by Jefferson and his followers, that forced the Congress to add one. After the inauguration of the Republic, almost every advance in what we now think of as liberal reform came from pressure by majorities insofar as we are able to distinguish them. It was the Federalists, under the leadership of those who most deeply distrusted the people, who wrote the Alien and Sedition Acts, and the Jeffersonian Democrats (who, as it turned out, were the majority) who erased these from the statute books. It was the majorities within the states that clamored for the reform of state constitutions, looking to broader suffrage, the end of property qualifications for officeholding, and the abolition of special privilege for favored denominations—in short, for broader political and religious freedom. It was the majority, too, who supported liberal immigration policy, the speedy admission of new western states, the broad suffrage, a generous western land policy, appropriations for public education, the abolition of imprisonment by debt, and many other reforms.

If once again we are assailed by the sobering suspicion that though Tocqueville did not always see clearly or justly what was before his eyes, no man of his generation had a surer vision for the distant future. Majority rule did not prove inimical to liberty or to justice during the nineteenth century, nor during the early years of the twentieth. In the Wilsonian era and with gathering force thereafter, the clouds drew across the bright horizons. I need not recapitulate what is familiar enough to most: the Espionage and Sedition Acts of the First World War; the petty reign of terror under Attorney General Palmer, the worst attorney general in American history until Mitchell; the gaggle of state laws designed to curb or outlaw subversive parties and subversive ideas; the misguided decisions of the Supreme Court, from *Abrams v. the United States* to *Dennis v. the United States* thirty years later, that so severely circumscribed the freedoms of the First Amendment; the tyrannies and atrocities committed by the Ku Klux Klan and many kindred organizations; Japanese relocation (the very euphemism is an affront); the antics of the un-American activities committees, state and federal alike; the Smith Act; the Mundt-Nixon Act; the McCarran Internal Security Act; the obscenities in the McCarthy crusade, supported by otherwise respectable men like Senator Taft; and perhaps the gravest threat to freedom and the integrity of the Republic since slavery itself, President Nixon's subversion of the Constitution and the Bill of Rights. Yet these same years saw the triumph and enactment of programs greatly enlarging the suffrage, liberating labor from the fetters of ancient common-law restrictions, ending child labor, underwriting lavish national support to elementary and higher education, to arts, and to science—in short, transforming a laissez-faire state into a welfare state, a revolution that went far toward making a government for the people, as earlier revolutions had made it a government by the people; and its ultimate design was a creation of that more just society which Tocqueville himself thought the special beauty of a democratic system. No one could doubt that the majority supported Wilson's New Freedom, and that Franklin Roosevelt's New Deal and Lyndon Johnson's Great Society were meant to enlarge the realm of liberty.

Though Tocqueville's analysis of the tyranny of the majority was profound, it was in its anticipation of the American scene misguided. Majorities did not, perhaps because they could not, impose either lasting or widespread conformity on the American mind or spirit, nor did they exercise tyranny over American opinion or conduct. Tocqueville knew, too, that when men turned to the state to enlarge democracy and enhance justice, they inevitably strengthened the centralized government and brought into being a giant bureaucracy. These, Tocqueville thought, were the implacable enemies of liberty. It is to this problem of the relation of the Leviathan state to liberty that I now turn.

TWO

The Price of a Just Society

It was the phenomenon of equality that most fascinated Tocqueville as he viewed the new American society, and this clearly because it so sharply differentiated the New World from the Old. His discussion of equality was therefore not only penetrating but elaborate. Justice, however, he took for granted, and when he did address himself to it, it was only briefly and in somewhat technical terms such as the operations of the jury system or the role of the courts. Curiously enough, his tribute to equality as a system that best embodies justice stands by itself. It is a brilliant and profound insight and one written with immense eloquence. It is, however, as we shall see, innocent of demonstration. It is an emotional conclusion rather than a reasoned one.

"When I survey this countless multitude of beings," wrote Tocqueville on almost the last page of the *Democracy*,

> shaped in each other's likeness, amid whom nothing rises and nothing falls, the sight of such universal uniformity saddens and chills me, and I am tempted to regret that state of society which has ceased to be. When the world was full of men of great importance and extreme insignificance, of great wealth and extreme poverty, of great learning and extreme ignorance, I turned aside from the latter to fix my observation on the former alone, who gratified my sympathies. But I admit that this gratification arose from my own weakness: it is because I am unable to see at once all that is around me that I am allowed thus

to select and separate the objects of my predilection from among so many others. Such is not the case with that Almighty and Eternal Being, whose gaze necessarily includes the whole of created things, and who surveys distinctly, though at once, mankind and man. We may naturally believe that it is not the singular prosperity of the few, but the greater well-being of all, which is most pleasing in the sight of the Creator and Preserver of men. What appears to me to be man's decline is to his eye advancement; what afflicts me is acceptable to him. A state of equality is perhaps less elevated, but it is more just; and its justice constitutes its greatness and its beauty.

Tocqueville put the matter somewhat more elaborately in a letter to his friend Eugene Stirfells when he said that men in a republic may develop less than those in other governments some of the noblest powers of the human mind. "It yet has a nobility of its own and that after all it may be God's will to spread a moderate amount of happiness over all men instead of heaping a large sum upon a few by allowing men a small minority to approach perfection."

Now before we can accept Tocqueville's conclusion distinguishing the feature of equality in America as justice, we must look a little more closely and a little more critically both to equality and to justice. As I observe Tocqueville's otherwise so scrupulous use of words, here it is important to note that he employs the terms *democracy* and *equality* interchangeably. So too, for that matter, do we. How much less ambiguous it would be if we confined the terms *democracy* or *democratic* to the political processes whereby men are governed, and used the term *equality* to mean the political, the social, the economic circumstances of those who govern and those who are governed.

Democracy, if we are stubborn, can be defined with some precision. Equality has so many meanings and connotations that it all but baffles either definition or description. The most prominent of these meanings are familiar enough, so I shall confine myself to listing them (each one of these deserves a book, really, and each of them, of course, has been written about at great length): equality in the sight of God and equality in the eyes of nature, the two meanings explicit in the Declaration of Independence; equality in the eyes of the law; equality in participation in government and politics; equality in the enjoyment of the benefits and protection that government confers, such as the problem of the interpretation of the "equal protection of the laws" clause of the Fourteenth Amendment, whether that is to be interpreted procedurally or substantively; equality in religion and religious worship; equality in access to education at every level; social equality, the condition that, to Tocqueville, took its most characteristic and most interesting form in the flourishing voluntary associations; and finally, and of growing importance, economic equality.

Collectively, these embraced equality of status and equality of opportunity, which might in time produce equality of conditions, while almost from the beginning the equality of status—that is, equality before the law and in politics and in religion, etc.—could be taken for granted by white Americans. To this extent Tocqueville's almost envious observation was accurate: "The great advantage of the Americans is that they have arrived at a state of democracy without having to endure a democratic revolution; and that they are born equal, instead of becoming so."

That was not quite true in the economic arena, even in the more pastoral, enlightened eighteenth century, and the paradox emerged early that social equalities encouraged economic inequalities; for social and political equality produced individualism, or encouraged it, and individualism in

turn instructed the average American that he could over-
come economic inequality by hard work or by luck or by
cunning or simply by moving to some more favorable
climate. It was this conviction, a conviction rooted in nature
and in human nature, that for so long mitigated popular
resentment against economic inequality, and indeed persuaded vast numbers of Americans to look upon economic
inequality with approval, an approval born of self-confi-
dence; and it is this attitude that explains the paradox that the
majority of Americans persisted in preferring private to
public enterprise and tolerated something like economic
classes while they resented and repudiated social classes.

In England, by contrast, certainly in the England where
social inequality was dramatized by economic inequality,
there was no such amelioration of class antagonisms. Thus
Tocqueville was not alone in preferring a rich and varied
social spectacle to one where nothing rises and nothing falls.
Most English and many Americans were uncomfortable in
the presence of "universal uniformity." But their discontent
manifested itself in very different ways, and the differences
go far to vindicate Tocqueville's insight that laws and habits
and customs and institutions are more important in the
formation of national character than either environment or
inheritance. In our own day the English have been prepared
to tolerate and even pay for an economic system that has
made for relative uniformity as long as they could retain a
social system that preserved class distinctions, and at least
some of the privileges of the upper class, if only the privilege
of upper-class speech. It is that, of course, which every
middle-class Englishman bankrupts and beggars himself
over by sending his children to what are there called public
schools, which are our private, so that they will learn the
proper accents, aware as they are of Orwell's terrible indict-

ment that every Englishman is branded on the tongue at birth.

In America, where social distinctions have always been negligible and economic distinctions somewhat more ostentatious, the people rejoiced in an economic system where fortunes rose and fell almost as a matter of course, but they insisted on a social system that was uniform and indiscriminating.

We are confronted here with a paradox that was, in the end, to undermine the validity of the Tocquevillian thesis of the interdependence of democracy and a just society in America; I mean, of course, slavery and the inability or the refusal of Americans to grant justice to the blacks. Tocqueville, who saw everything, saw that slavery permeated the whole social, economic, and moral life of the South, and that it decreed injustice to the free as well as to the enslaved blacks. He predicted that in the end slavery would be the rock on which the Union would founder. Yet oddly enough, he did not concern himself directly with the clamorous challenge to his thesis that the democratic society was a just society.

Less surprising, for it was an accepted attitude in the nineteenth century, was his failure to take note of the palpable inequality of women, and not just political inequality, but legal, economic, social, educational, and moral subordination.

Slavery was eventually ended, though not by the arguments of reason, of morals, or of economy, but by those of force. It is still true that the most important and the most spectacular constitutional decision in our history was made at Appomattox. Yet even this did not bring justice to the blacks. In a sense it spread and nationalized existing injustices, for by detaching racism from slavery, and then through a long series of court decisions denying blacks that equal protection of the laws guaranteed in the Fourteenth Amendment, the end of slavery seemed to exempt injustice from the reach of the law, and even gave it a measure of respectability.

Slavery metamorphosed into what Gunnar Myrdal rightly called "the American dilemma," and for another century the descendants of those who had fought for slavery and those who had fought against it learned to live with relative comfort with that dilemma. Interestingly, it took a Swede to dramatize it and force its attention upon us. What slavery represented, in short, was not merely the most glaring exception to Tocqueville's just society, but the most resistant. When in his second inaugural address Franklin Roosevelt spoke of one-third of the nation ill-housed, ill-clad, and ill-nourished—and he might have added ill-schooled, ill-protected, and ill—a substantial part of that third, approximately one-third of it, was black. Today, following the vast influx of Puerto Ricans and Mexicans, both legal and illegal, the proportion of ethnic minorities below the poverty line is substantially larger than it was in 1937.

Injustice to minority ethnic groups is no longer, as it was in Tocqueville's day, an official policy. Indeed, it is not a policy at all. But perhaps its very inadvertence dramatizes the pervasiveness and the stubbornness that permits social and economic injustice to flourish in the face of the law, in the face of official policies designed to give substance to promises of justice.

As Tocqueville did not acknowledge the extent to which slavery undermined his theory of the connection of democracy with justice, so he did not seem to realize how deeply the institution of slavery qualified liberty even for those who were free. Surprisingly enough, he failed to take to heart the familiar admonition that those who would enslave others must first enslave themselves; or to echo Jefferson's observation that slavery was a perpetual exercise of the most boisterous of passions, the most unremitting despotism on the one part and the most degrading submission on the other. History had acquainted Tocqueville with the dangers of power, and he knew well the poison of the passion of a Robespierre or a Napoleon. Implicitly, if not explicitly, he anticipated Lord Acton's aphorism that power corrupts and absolute power, which of course the slaveowner did have over the slave, corrupts absolutely. But he did not clearly see that the passion for power nurtured in the school of slavery was bound to linger on even after the end of slavery, and that this was incompatible with liberty.

Perhaps more important is the question of justice. Justice, Tocqueville concluded, is a special virtue which most clearly vindicates democracy. "A state of equality," he wrote, "is perhaps less elevated, but it is more just; and its justice constitutes its greatness and its beauty." How does the verdict stand now? Ours is politically, and to a large extent socially, an equalitarian society. Is it a just society? Just as a Benjamin Franklin or a Theodore Parker or a Lester Ward or a Jane Addams envisioned it? Just as a Jefferson, a Lincoln, a Franklin Roosevelt, a Lyndon Johnson sought to make it? Is it just by that most elementary of all tests, equal justice under the law? Or do we have today one law for the rich and powerful, and another for the poor and helpless? One for the establishment, and another for what Parker called the "perishing and dangerous classes of society"?

It was to study the American penal and prison system that Tocqueville and his friend Beaumont came to America, and it is sobering to recall that they thought the American experiment a model for the Old World. What would Tocqueville think today of the prisons whose very existence humane judges have pronounced an obscenity, or that penal code which condemns one man to prison for twenty years for an act which is not even a crime in a neighboring state? The two states here are West Virginia and Ohio, and the crimes—crime in one and not in another—have to do with sexual conduct. Would he find that those who corrupt themselves through drugs and those who corrupt society through corporate skulduggery suffer the same penalties? Would he find that those guilty of crime in the streets and those guilty of causing disability or death by the neglect of elementary sanitary codes at mine heads, or by the pollution of water and air, are given the same sentence? Would he find that white and black alike suffer the same punishments for the same crimes, or that rich women and poor have an equal claim on medical care in pregnancy or in rejecting pregnancy? Would he find that those who evade laws requiring military service and those who grossly violate the laws of war on a massive scale are equally reprobated? And would he find that the principles laid down at the Nuremberg trials and the Tokyo war crime trials apply equally to American war crimes and war criminals? Would he not find that those who lie about their welfare status are duly punished, but those who perjure themselves out of an arrogance that sets them above the law are covered with honors and rewards? Would he find that those who betray a fiduciary trust in private affairs are regarded with that contempt which they merit, that those who violate the sacred trust of high office—indeed the highest office—are not only immune from punishment, but rewarded by an admiring society for their treason?

Over the past quarter century, our courts have gone far to provide equal justice under the law and equal protection of the laws. It was a recognition that laws ordaining capital punishment were not impartially applied among white and black that led to the suspension of the death penalty. Have courts and juries now become color-blind, so that we can safely restore the death penalty?

It was a realization that the doctrine of separate but equal educational facilities was a fraud and that, to quote Chief Justice Warren, "separate educational facilities are inherently unequal," that dictated the historic decision of *Brown v. Board of Education*. Have we now so completely erased social barriers and racial discrimination in schools and achieved an equality so sophisticated that we can afford to see this decision ignored or nullified?

It was a recognition that the poor and the outcast were not assured the same protection of the law as the rich and the privileged that led to the Miranda decision and those many elaborations upon it designed to provide equal protection of the laws and due process of the law for all, the "perishing and dangerous" as well as for the privileged. Have we sufficiently guaranteed equal justice and a fair trial for all, so that we can now dispense with Miranda? We were vindictive toward those who refused to fight in a war in Vietnam that they thought unjust and immoral, but we do not always prosecute those agents of the CIA and the FBI, whose business it is to enforce the law, for the countless crimes they committed— committed with official approval, to be sure—nor did we prosecute those who improperly gave their approval. Is there one justice for the citizen and another for those who regard themselves as rulers above the law, not servants of the people and of the law?

Inequality before the law is the most pernicious of all manifestations of injustice because it undermines the foundations of law, of government, and of morality. Injustices are even more pervasive and more widely burdensome in the economic than in the legal arena. There we find discriminational access to jobs, education, housing, health and medical care, and a lack of security and dignity for the old and the poor.

In many of these areas, justice is taken for granted in most of the civilized nations of the globe, certainly in the Western world, but it is denied or withheld in the United States. If nations without the resources of the United States and without her long experience with democracy and equality can reconcile the demands of justice with those of liberty and adjust their ancient institutions of class and privilege to the requirements of the welfare state, why is it so difficult for the United States to do so? Why do we choose to ignore the constitutional admonition to promote the general welfare and the constitutional authority to provide for the general welfare? How interesting that those who are most attitudinary in their construction of the executive power or the war power clauses tend to be strict constructionists when it comes to the general welfare clauses.

Why do Americans, almost alone of democratic peoples, appear to assume that general welfare is repugnant to private welfare as public is to private enterprise? Certainly there is little in the experience of our sister democracies in Western Europe or elsewhere, in what was once a British Common-wealth of nations, to justify these fears. Concern for the environment and the preservation of natural resources for posterity has not discouraged German industrial prosperity. Socialized medicine has not deprived the British either of first-rate medical care or of liberty. Cradle to grave social security has not dried up Norwegian or Swedish incentives—quite the contrary, I should think, if we view their economy and their intellectual activities. The establishment of a humane penal code and prison system has not increased crime in Sweden. The elimination of urban slums in Denmark has not come at the expense of either beauty or charm, and certainly not at the expense of the poor. Culture has not yielded to vulgarity with the subsidy of the opera and the theater in Vienna and Milan, subsidies far greater than anything given the Metropolitan, by the way. Public ownership of railroads in Switzerland has not led to chaos in transportation in that country, and private initiative still appears to flourish in the welfare states of Australia and New Zealand.

Would Tocqueville, who was persuaded that the growth of governmental activity was inimical to liberty, interject that men would almost always choose equality over liberty? Would he have been alarmed at the emergence of the modern welfare state? What he wrote quite privately in his *Recollections* is, I think, to the point:

> The more I study the former state of the world, and indeed even when I see the modern world in greater detail, when I consider the prodigious diversity found there, not just in the laws but in the principles of the laws, and the different forms that the right of property has taken . . . I am tempted to the belief that what are called necessary institutions are only institutions to which one is accustomed, and that in matters of social constitution the field of possibilities is much wider than people living within each society imagine.

Would he not have reflected, and reflection was his special forte, that what we call "the welfare state" might indeed be one of those different forms that the right of property has taken, whose possibilities are wider than society has imagined? Might he not have concluded that this was indeed the way in which a just society, which he thought the *summa bonum* of history, was to be achieved, and that the ability of his own nation and that of England, which he loved next to France, to achieve this was a tribute to a resourcefulness they had failed to display in his own lifetime? He had seen something of that resourcefulness in America and rejoiced in it. A great many of his contemporaries, he observed in the conclusion of *Democracy in America,* wished to preserve some of the privileges they had heretofore enjoyed and to transplant them to their New World. "I apprehend," he added, "that such men are wasting their time and their strength in virtuous but unprofitable efforts. The object is not to retain the peculiar advantages which the inequality of conditions bestows upon mankind, but to secure the new benefits which equality may supply. We have not to seek to make ourselves like our progenitors, but to strive to work out that species of greatness and happiness which is our own.... The nations of our time," he concluded, and this is over a century and a half ago, "cannot prevent the conditions of men from becoming equal; but it depends upon themselves whether the principle of equality is to lead them to servitude or freedom, to knowledge or barbarism, to prosperity or to wretchedness."

A final observation on aspects and implications of justice is, I think, in order. There are two aspects of justice that Tocqueville does not consider which we too are inclined to overlook, particularly when we think of justice as Professor Rawles of Harvard does, almost exclusively as fairness. These two are justice to posterity and justice to mankind elsewhere on the globe.

It is difficult to exaggerate the commitment to posterity of the Founding Fathers. Thus Tom Paine, for example, who had only come over in 1774, but was very much one of the Founding Fathers, observed: "Does not concern of a day, a year, or an age, posterity is involved in the contest." (It was a contest of independence.) Thus a Pennsylvania Framer, John Dickinson: "Honor, justice, and humanity forbid us to surrender that freedom which our innocent posterity have a right to receive from us." Thus George Mason of Gunston Hall down in Virginia, who wrote the Virginia Bill of Rights, admonished his children to transmit to posterity those sacred rights in which they were themselves born. Or John Adams, writing the evening he had voted for the Declaration of Independence: "Through all the gloom I see the rays of ravishing light and glory. Posterity will triumph in this day's transaction even though we may not." Or here is Dr. Benjamin Rush down in Philadelphia, another of the Constitution's signers: "I was aware constantly, I was animated constantly, by a belief that I was acting for the benefit of the whole world and of posterity." I could go on and on. "I like the dreams of the future better than the history of the past," said Jefferson. That was logical enough, for America was indeed the future and it was posterity who would realize, so they thought, those dreams that the revolutionary generation had fought to secure and to preserve.

That our own generation has largely lost its faith or even its belief in posterity seems to be self-evident. The natural resources of the country belong to no one generation, but as Jefferson put it, to our descendants to the thousands and thousands of generations. Imagine any president today speculating on a thousand generations. I think the only speculation of the future is, "Can we balance the budget in two years?" That is about as far ahead as anyone cares to think. It was the same Jefferson who proposed not only rewriting every constitution each generation (and with that passion for figuring things out, he figured that each generation came to maturity at precisely twenty and one-half years) but also repudiating all public debts each generation on the ground that the earth belonged to the living, not the dead, and that no one generation had a right to pass debts down to future generations. I do not know if he was confident that each generation would manage to accumulate them on their own, but in any event he did not think this was the way to treat posterity.

Now we ravage the resources, which belong not to us but to the future, with heedless selfishness: destroying the soil, the forests, and the inland waters; killing life in the oceans; polluting the air and endangering the ozone that protects us from the rays of the burning sun; loudly and almost unanimously—though the environmentalists would not agree with that—echoing Madame Pompadour, "After us, the deluge." We pile up insensate debts for our children to pay, although there is no evidence that they will get anything for their money. We know that atomic leaks can poison the atmosphere that our children will breathe, but do little to end that threat. We know, too, that a nuclear war would end civilization and perhaps life on our planet, but until recently we persisted in building ever larger arsenals of nuclear weapons, which might have clamored at some time to be used. How to explain the evaporation of that sense of fiduciary obligation which animated our forebears?

We have pretty much lost our faith in America as the land of the future. We have no faith in millennialism, nor few of the illusions we once had that America was itself Utopia. We have pretty well abandoned the notion of progress except in the scientific and technological areas, and we are afraid of innovation in the public or in the political. How sobering it is to reflect that every fundamental constitutional and political institution that we now live with was invented before the year 1800, and that not one has been invented since the year 1800. That political fecundity, that political resourcefulness, that ingenuity, that imagination which dominated the Age of Enlightenment of the Founding Fathers disappeared and has not so far been revived. Perhaps most fundamental is the fact that with the threat of nuclear warfare hanging over us, however diminished that threat may now seem, we no longer have any genuine confidence that there will be any posterity to take care of, certainly not to the thousands and thousands of generations. This may well prove to be the ultimate self-fulfilling prophecy.

In contrast, the generation that created the American commonwealth was concerned not only with posterity but with mankind. That was an Enlightenment preoccupation, for the Enlightenment was based upon the assumption, the whole of the Newtonian worldview was based on the assumption, that mankind was everywhere the same, governed everywhere by the same fundamental laws. It was everyone, not just all Americans, who was entitled to life, liberty, and happiness; the rights for which Americans fought were the rights of mankind, and it was a special mission of America first to vindicate those rights, then to spread them throughout the globe; not, by the way, to spread them by force, but by example. Thus Jefferson's wonderfully appropriate letter, the last that he ever wrote, just as the pen fell from his lifeless hand:

> Reasserting the significance of the American experiment, may it be to the world a signal of arousing men to burst the chains under which monkish ignorance and superstition had persuaded them to bind themselves, and to assume the blessings and securities of self-government. All eyes are opened or opening to the rights of man. The general mass of mankind has not been born with saddles on their backs, nor a favored few booted and spurred ready to ride them legitimately, by the grace of God. These are grounds of hopes for others, for ourselves, that the annual return of the day July Fourth forever refresh our recollections of these rights and the undiminished devotion to them.

Jefferson and his associates, deeply read as they were in history, were persuaded that freedom could not survive in a world dominated by tyranny, that a peaceful nation could not flourish in a world made up of predatory powers, that a just society could not prosper in the midst of widespread injustice. When they reflected on freedom they hoped to enlarge its boundaries everywhere. When they reflected on slavery they confessed, in the words of Jefferson, "Can the liberties of a nation be thought secure when we have removed their only firm basis, a conviction in the minds of the people that these liberties are the gift of God? They are not to be violated but with His wrath? Indeed, I tremble for my country when I reflect that God is just; that His justice cannot sleep forever. . . . The Almighty hath no attribute which can take side with us in such a contest." ("With us" meant the slaveholding whites.)

A people's character and a people's policies are, I think, of a piece, for policy reflects character. You cannot have justice at home if we impose or encourage injustice abroad. In Tocqueville's day, Americans displayed a double standard for freedom and slavery. During the past quarter century, we have fallen once again into not so much a double standard as a dual and a contradictory policy, one of advancing civil rights and liberties on the domestic front, but refusing these to many peoples internationally who do not see fit to subscribe to our policies. As we closed our eyes during the Cold War, we closed minds to the greatest revolution in human history, that revolution of two-thirds of the peoples of the globe, seeking, to use Jefferson's phrase, "through blood and slaughter their long-lost liberties." We still do not make justice or the welfare of the people the test of our support or of our hostility to the people and the nations of India and China, of Africa, of much of South America, and almost all of Central America. Instead of asking what is right and just for them, we ask what is convenient and flattering for us. That was why for a quarter of a century we adamantly refused to admit the largest and oldest nation of the globe, the People's Republic of China, to the fellowship of nations, why we supported not the people but the colonels in Greece and Spain and Portugal, and the military dictators in Cuba and Guatemala and Brazil and Chile, and *tilted* (to use that marvelous word) toward Pakistan.

Until we can enlarge our concept of freedom and of justice to embrace all peoples, our commitment to justice must be suspect. Should we not seek to revive something of that deep obligation to posterity and to mankind by that standard of nobility and magnanimity which, as all the Founding Fathers knew, was best expressed by Pericles in his great funeral oration to describe what he set up as the glory of Athens? "In doing good we are the exact opposite of the rest of mankind. We secure our friends, not by accepting favors but by doing them, and so we are naturally more firm in our attachments, for we are anxious as creditors to cement by kind offices our relations toward our friends. We are alone among mankind in doing men benefits, not on calculations of self-interest, but in the fearless confidence of freedom."

THREE
Centralization and Democracy

The central problem not only of democracy but of government itself is the reconciliation of liberty and order—who shall bridle Behemoth, who shall curb Leviathan? It is the oldest, as it is the most difficult, problem in politics. It is a question that by its very nature cannot be fully answered, but I think we may say that in modern history it has been more reassuringly explored by democratic processes than by any other. This problem must be reflected against the background of Tocqueville's somewhat paradoxical observation that where liberty is a product of art, government and governmental centralization is a process of nature; while the first is to be achieved only by the most ardent and arduous effort, the second advances like gravity itself.

Tocqueville devoted the whole of his intellectual activities to the cultivation of the art of advancing and protecting liberty, that is, the art of controlling nature. For illumination of this fundamental problem he looked to America.

In the Old World, as he saw it, nature had triumphed over art. Then, to use Emerson's wonderful phrase, "History had baked their cake." But in America, and this was of course the vision that animated Jefferson and his disciples, art could triumph over nature, for America had come late on the stage of history and was not the slave of history but might be its master. "Shake not your raw and bloody bones at me," Jefferson used to say. What he meant was that here in the

New World, where natural and human resources seemed limitless, where there were no military pressures to require the subordination of liberty to security, and where an enlightened citizenry was free of the tyrannies of the past, men might achieve liberty without exposing themselves to the dangers of turbulence or to the threat of license and ruin. Clearly America was not only the best of all laboratories in which to conduct the experiment of self-government, but the one where the elusive secret of the reconciliation of liberty and order might at last be discovered.

So Tocqueville thought, as Jefferson and his colleagues had thought, but was it indeed? Was art really auspicious? How did it happen then that Americans had contrived for themselves the benefit of liberty and had imposed slavery on others? Did not the defense of slavery implacably require a government strong enough to set limits to freedom, not only for the blacks but also for those whites who were opposed to slavery, as governments did, of course, in every southern state?

Moreover, Montesquieu, whom Tocqueville admired above all other statesmen and philosophers, had demonstrated, he did not just submit, that because size was everywhere the enemy of freedom, and that it was the enemy in proportion to the size, then the larger the empire, the more unavoidable the despotism. A monarchy, a monarchical state, he said, ought to be of moderate extent and could avoid a despotism; a small state could form itself into a republic and only a small state. He concluded that if it be the natural property of small states to be governed as a republic, of middling ones to be subject to a monarchy, and of large empires to be swayed by a despotic prince, the consequence is that the spirit of the state will alter in proportion as it contracts or extends its limits. Now this was, almost all philosophers agreed, a law of history, but it was a very alarming law for Americans, for they had already vastly expanded their limits, and more expansion, as we know, lay ahead. Could they expect to be exempt from the operation of the laws of history? As they looked about them in Tocqueville's day, could they find confirmation of Montesquieu or refutation?

Among Western nations only Russia was as large as the United States, and Russia was a despotism. The Spanish empire was larger than the United States could ever expect to be, even after she had fulfilled her Manifest Destiny, or it was at least until the revolutions in Latin America broke it up, after which the empire was ruled despotically. Indeed, everywhere on the globe the large empires, the large states, seemed to have a special weakness for, or strength for, despotism.

Jefferson had asserted that none of the predictions, however, of Montesquieu applied to the United States, for it was unique. The American people were not to be enslaved by history; their destiny was to make history. So he said to John Adams that before the establishment of the American states, nothing was known to history but men of the Old World, crowded with limits and steeped in the vices which that situation generated. A government adapted to such men would be one thing, but it would be very different adapted to men of the United States. Here everyone may have land to labor for himself, everyone has interest in the support of law and order. Such men may safely reserve to themselves a degree of freedom that in the hands of the rulers of Europe would be instantly perverted to the demolition and destruction of everything, public and private alike. Even better, Jefferson's friend Madison demonstrated in Number Ten of the *Federalist Papers* not only that size could be reconciled with liberty, but also that it could be made an effective instrument for the advancement of liberty.

Oddly enough, Tocqueville paid no attention to Jefferson. He is mentioned only once in one of the appendixes to *Democracy*, and though Tocqueville knew the *Federalist Papers*, he paid no attention to Number Ten. (Perhaps not so odd. Charles Beard "discovered" Number Ten in 1913. It had not gotten very much attention before that time.)

The question that Montesquieu posed and which Jefferson and Madison answered in one way and Tocqueville in another persisted and is with us now in different form. Geographically, America grew to continental dimensions, but technology and science canceled out the traditional implications of such growth and even reversed them. But technology and science have carried with them their own growth. Size is not just a phenomenon or area of population, but of economy and of culture and, as Tocqueville dimly saw, of power.

How did Americans manage to limit and control the perils of centralization in the nineteenth century? How did they cope with them in the twentieth? How can they hope to surmount them in the twenty-first? Can they survive the dangers of centralization induced by that industrial economy which so profoundly transformed Jefferson's agrarian republic, that military power which he labored to banish from the American scene, that government which he had thought would always remain limited and simple?

Let us listen to Tocqueville as he expounds his thesis. He is applying the familiar principle that history is philosophy teaching by example, a principle taken for granted by almost everyone until the notion that history is a separate discipline came along in the mid-eighteenth and early nineteenth century. Once again he finds his examples in the history of the Old World and applies their lessons confidently to the New. There are three tenets to his thesis: one is that central-ization is both inevitable and irresistible; two, that the danger is not so much in centralization of authority as in centraliza-tion of administration; and three, that such centralization leads to tyranny. Everyone, he asserts,

> will perceive that for the last half-century, centralization has everywhere been growing up in a thousand different ways. Wars, revolutions, conquests, have served to promote it: all men have labored to increase it. In the course of the same period, . . . their notions, interests, and passions have been infinitely diversified; but all have by some means or other sought to centralize. This instinctive centralization has been the only settled point amidst the extreme mutability of their lives and their thoughts.

And he said he could not conceive that a nation could live and prosper without a powerful centralization of government. "But I am of the opinion that a central administration enervates the nations in which it exists by incessantly dimin-ishing their public spirit." This inner compulsion to central-ization, Tocqueville argued, is particularly powerful in democratic societies, where there are no forces or interests strong enough to resist it or to offer an alternative to the power of government. Clearly, for service in the central administration is or will become the only magnet for ambi-tious men, centralization is part of the tide of democracy. Far from fearing a centralized administration then, Tocqueville observed, they will welcome it, for they are centralizing it for their own benefit, not for the benefit of the nation. After all, among the public men of great democracies there are hardly any but men of great disinterestedness or extreme mediocrity who seek to oppose the centralization of government. The former are scarce, the latter are powerless.

Nor are these the only reasons centralization is bound to triumph in a democracy: as Tocqueville wrote, because democracy demands equality of treatment, it is easier and more desirable to centralize the administration of laws, and because in a democracy men are passionately devoted to their own pursuits and advantages, they will resent some forms of government interference, but when they need special help or favors they will clamor for governmental assistance regardless of their commitment to individuals.

How prescient Tocqueville was in this, in seeing that though individualism dictates freedom from government restraint or government intervention, there is always an exception to that rule; each individual man or individual interest craves government's assistance in the particular concern in which he is engaged and seeks to draw upon the influence of the government for his own benefit, although he would resist it on all other occasions. If a large number of men, he wrote, applies this particular exception to a great variety of different purposes, the sphere of the central power extends itself imperceptibly in all directions although everyone wishes it to be circumscribed. And thus a democratic government increases its power simply by the fact of its permanence. It may be asserted that the older a democratic community is, the more centralized will its government become.

The interdependence of despotism and centralization in the Old World was, of course, a fact of history. It was a fact in the France of Louis XIV, the Prussia of Frederick the Great, the Denmark of the Fredericks and the Christians, and the Russia of Catherine. This did not need to be demonstrated, it was axiomatic. But what of America, which had no princes and no despots? America, said Tocqueville, would not be an exception. It would indeed provide a new kind of despotism, for "the species of oppression by which democratic nations are menaced is unlike anything which ever before existed in the world: our contemporaries will find no prototype of it in their memories." It is one where a vast "multitude of men ... incessantly endeavoring to procure the petty and paltry pleasures with which they glut their lives" are prepared to concede to a central government immense and tutelary power. "That power," he said, with somewhat mild exaggeration,

> is absolute, minute, regular, provident, and mild.... It seeks on the contrary to keep them in perpetual childhood: it is well content that the people should rejoice, provided they think of nothing but rejoicing. For their happiness such a government willingly labors, but it chooses to be the sole agent and the only arbiter of that happiness: it provides for their security, foresees and supplies their necessities, facilitates their pleasures, manages their principal concerns, directs their industry, regulates the descent of property, and subdivides their inheritances— what remains, but to spare them all the care of thinking and all the trouble of living?

Such a power, he concluded in his extraordinary anticipation of some aspects of the welfare state, does not destroy, but it prevents existence: "It does not tyrannize, but it compresses, enervates, extinguishes, and stupefies a people, till each nation is reduced to be nothing better than a flock of timid and industrious animals, of which the government is the shepherd."

And then came the cynical conclusion that applies, I think accurately enough, to the Italy and Germany of the mid-twentieth century:

I have always thought the servitude . . . which I have just described, might be combined more easily than is commonly believed with some of the outward forms of freedom; and that it might even establish itself under the wing of the sovereignty of the people. Our contemporaries are constantly excited by two conflicting passions; they want to be led and they wish to remain free. . . . They devise a sole, tutelary, and all-powerful form of government, but elected by the people. They combine the principle of centralization and that of popular sovereignty; this gives them a respite; they console themselves for being in tutelage by the reflection that they have chosen their own guardians.

Historically, Tocqueville was amply justified in his fears of centralization. For centuries strong, highly centralized governments had been the most effective instruments of tyranny. By contrast, some degree of freedom flourished precisely where the central authority was relatively weak—the Low Countries, the Swiss cantons, eighteenth-century Britain, and the American colonies. He was right, too, tragically right, in his vision of the perversion of the principles of republicanism and of democracy that were to stain the history of those nations that in our own time invoke democracy to justify totalitarian dictatorship and to excuse the most monstrous of crimes against humanity.

But were generalizations and prophecies based on some centuries of Old World history valid for America? Nothing in the American scene, from independence to the Jacksonian era, supported such a dire conclusion. Five major forces first stimulated, then required, the centralization of authority in administration that Tocqueville anticipated with such grave misgivings: first, the Constitution, transformed by the Fourteenth Amendment and eventually interpreted by the courts to extend the mantle of federal protection to all persons and corporations in the United States; second, the economy as transformed by the industrial, scientific, and technological revolutions of the past century; third, the decline of many of those habits, practices, and institutions of localism that had long operated as countervailing forces against centralization; fourth, the felt necessity of saving the natural resources of the country from destruction or exhaustion; and fifth, the importunate demands of world power and of national security, which increasingly took a military character.

The primary purpose of the Constitution of 1787, it should be remembered, was precisely to form a more perfect Union. That meant a Union stronger than that which had existed so tenuously under the Articles of Confederation. Once that Constitution was ratified and the new government established, all the forces making for nationalism and centralization gravitated to it. It was, of course, the Fourteenth Amendment that, by extending the blanket of national protection of all rights, privileges, and liberties of Americans against deprivation or denial by states, inaugurated the fundamental revolution of our constitutional system. Eventually it became the chief instrument for nationalizing social, economic, and traditional private and civil rights.

Second, in the Old World, political centralization commonly preceded and was the instrument of economic change. In the United States, national centralization has been in very large measure a function of economic change, a function of the economy. That authority of the federal government to regulate all interstate commerce, corporations, currency, banking, immigration, etc., was there from the beginning. But even Hamilton's genius was not sufficient to persuade the federal government to exercise these and other powers. It was not until the 1880s that the Congress got around to legislating effectively in these areas. The authority to give substance to the general welfare clause was there, I think, at the beginning. It required, however, the greatest of depressions, needless to say that of 1929, and the New Deal, to persuade the Congress to sponsor a welfare state program long common in the nations of Western Europe and of the British Commonwealth. When business and industry were small and local they could be regulated by local authority. As they became national they called for national regulation. So, too, with quasi-economic activities, such as television. Politics did not impose centralized regulation upon business. Business imperatively required regulation by politics.

The third factor making for the concentration of authority in modern America is the decline of the effectiveness of those countervailing forces that operated so powerfully in Tocqueville's day, a decline which shows no sign of abating. As problems become insoluble by local action, many of the functions once assigned to towns and cities have been taken over by the states and, in our own time, by the national government. (Even in New England the town meeting lingers on as a romantic anachronism.) What is true politically is even more true economically. The major interests—farming, cattle-raising, mining, railroads, oil, aviation, you can go on and on—still speak the language of localism, of laissez-faire, but work ceaselessly for support from the national government. Education is still controlled by the states, but national educational organizations have imposed on it their pattern of uniformity. Colleges and universities look with increasing success to the federal government for financial support.

There are now more private associations by far than in the 1830s, but most of these strive for national character and national constituency. Historically indeed, one of the major functions of the private voluntary association was that it cut across state and regional boundary lines and contributed powerfully to nationalism. Thus labor unions, churches, reform movements, organizations that represent the interests of veterans, of the aged, of women and children, and countless other groups, commonly agitate for national support through federal legislation. They do not moderate the forces of centralization, but rather invigorate them.

The fourth development making for the expansion of federal authority is a product of the realization that the resources of the nation are not infinite, one of the greatest psychological revolutions in the whole of our history and one that has come really only in the last twenty years or so, as we so long deluded ourselves that our resources were infinite and that therefore no intervention was called for. It is clear now that neither voluntary self-restraint nor state intervention can possibly save them from exploitation and destruction. West Virginia is not prepared to end strip mining, nor Ohio to stop pollution of the Ohio River, nor Minnesota to require mining companies to cease dumping tons of dangerous chemicals in Lake Superior. Nor can states be trusted to set effective standards to prevent deadly poisons from breeder power plants. Individuals will not conserve oil by buying small cars or driving at fifty-five miles per hour. Nor will they voluntarily give up the profits from killing seals or dolphins any more than in the past they were prepared to forgo the pleasures of killing buffalo and carrier pigeons. Belatedly, most Americans have come to realize that if nature is to be saved for posterity it must be the national government or some international organization that will do the job.

The fifth major development making for centralization emerged during the Civil War. I mean, of course, the importunate demands of the military and the rise of America to world power, which can be dated from the 1890s. In the last half century we have had three fighting wars, the Cold

War—which lasted forty years—and a series of paramilitary operations around the globe. All have powerfully accelerated that centralization inherent in the very existence of the military.

These developments and pressures, operating ceaselessly like the force of gravity, have indeed brought about a centralization of authority and of administration of a formidable character, one of which we might say only a Hamilton among the Founding Fathers could have foreseen or would have approved. Has that process, which has culminated in our own day, vindicated Tocqueville's predictions of the malign influence of centralization on democracy and on liberty? Has it led to tyranny? That Tocqueville's thesis has been amply and tragically vindicated in the history of the Old World is clear; I need not elaborate on that—a Mussolini in Italy, a Franco in Spain, a Hitler in Germany, a Stalin in Russia, a Sukarno in Indonesia, a Castro in Cuba, and so on. But is the thesis, which so far has not been vindicated by our history, valid?

It would be folly to maintain that there are no grave dangers in federal centralization, or that there are not losses as well as gains in the concentration of political authority in Washington that has now been going on for the past half century. But those who today declaim most eloquently against big government as the enemy of freedom and enterprise do not come into the court of history with clean hands. It was, after all, the states that maintained slavery and the national government that abolished it. It was the states that ignored or repudiated the plain mandate of the Fourteenth and Fifteenth Amendments for almost a century, and, through the Civil Rights Acts of the 1970s and 1980s, it was the national government that actually enforced them. In the realm of what we call civil liberties, too, it is the states rather than the nation that have been the most conspicuous and consistent offenders. It is the federal government that has expanded civil liberties by legislation and by administrative enforcement, and it is for the most part the federal courts that have protected them and enlarged them.

Just as the notion of the tyranny of the majority is, in a sense, an elitist notion, so too is the fear of a government that is big enough to cope with the problems that most deeply affect majorities. Certainly it would be asking a great deal to ask blacks to accept the conclusion that the states have been the guardians of their freedom and the central government the enemy. It would be asking a great deal to ask women, so long denied the vote, even now denied equal rights before the law and in the economy, to believe that they should look to the states for reform rather than to the Congress, or to local rather than to federal courts. Suffrage came, after all, through a federal amendment. Equal rights, if it comes, will come either through the guarantees of the equal protection clause of the Fourteenth Amendment or through a new amendment. A long series of decisions protecting the interests of women from *Miller v. Oregon* back in 1908 to *Roe v. Wade,* the abortion decision of 1973, came from the federal courts. It would be asking a great deal to ask labor to accept the proposition that it was better off with the states than with the nation, with a weak national government rather than one that was vigorous and creative. In the twentieth century, certainly it is the federal Congress that has written successive charters of labor freedom, from the Clayton Antitrust Act of 1914 to the Wagner Act of 1935 and the Medicare Act of 1965. And it is the Congress that finally put an end to the disgrace of child labor, inaugurated a program of social security on a national scale, and ruled effectively to end racial discrimination in employment at every level. It would be asking a great deal to ask conservationists to accept the conclusion that they should look to the states or perhaps to private enterprise to preserve the natural resources of the nation for posterity, to end strip mining, or the exploitation of offshore oil, or the pollution of the waters of oceans and lakes and rivers, to save the redwoods of California or the grazing lands of Wyoming or, for that matter, the ducks and geese that fly over Missouri. I refer, as those of you familiar with our constitutional history know, to the great case of *Missouri v. Holland*, which enabled the United States government to do by treaty what it could not do by law and save migratory birds and a lot of other things from the depredations of hunters off-season.

We cannot eliminate danger to freedom from centralization of government nor to democracy from bigness. But by returning to the first principles we can, if we are wise and prudent, mitigate the impact of bigness and avoid the dangers of centralization. First, we must rid ourselves of the curious notion that the choice in allocating authority to local, state, or national governments is somehow a moral one. It is, thanks to the philosophy of our constitutional system, preeminently a practical one. For in our system all power inheres in the people as a whole, who are sovereign and who delegate political and administrative authority to those governments that they think best fitted to exercise it. Logically, no one government—local, state, or national—is closer to the people than any other. The great Justice Story stated this with characteristic clarity in one of the chapters of his magisterial commentaries on the Constitution:

> If the people withdraw power from the state and give it to the nation, it must be presumed to be because they deem it more useful for themselves, more for the common benefit and

common protection than to leave it where it had been heretofore deposited. Why should a power in the hands of one functionary be differently construed in the hands of another if, in each case, the same object is everywhere in view, the safety of the people. The state governments have no right to assume that power is more safe or more useful with them than with the general government, that they have a higher capacity and a more honest desire to preserve the rights and liberties of the people than the general government. The object of government is justice, freedom, and safety. We should not, out of a misguided sentiment, assume that local governments are more sensitive to justice or freedom than national, and certainly we clearly recognize that they are incompetent to provide for the common defense and desperately invoke the national aid even in day-by-day business of protecting the public safety.

We have learned, too, that local administration does not necessarily function more honestly, effectively, or economically than national, a lesson James Bryce pointed out a century ago in his *American Commonwealth* when he argued that state and city governments were the most conspicuous failures of American democracy. The decentralization of administration has not in fact contributed to the decline of bureaucracy. After all, in the past years the federal civil service has remained pretty much the same, while state and local authorities and civil service have almost tripled in size and in cost. Nor is it at all clear that decentralization has encouraged an intangible but significant value of a livelier participation in the concerns of government. The evidence to be drawn from the statistics of voting in local, state, and national elections would certainly support a very different conclusion. Almost everywhere the percentage of voting in the national elections is higher than that in local and in state.

Nor is it true, as Jefferson and Madison could assert in the

Kentucky and Virginia Resolutions of 1798, that it is the state governments that are the staunchest guardians of freedom against the usurpations of the national. Even in the lifetime of these two great humanitarians and libertarians, states' rights were duly invoked to protect slavery and to deny freedom to those who criticized slavery. Over the years it is centralization that has been enlisted in the task of curbing what Walt Whitman called the "unending audacity of elected persons" and of preserving liberty from the attacks by the states. Historically, most legislation subversive of freedom has come up from state or local authorities. It is these that take upon themselves authority to remove offending books from libraries, censor offending films, and penalize offending associations. It is the states that require loyalty oaths, impose flag salutes on school children, and have excluded blacks from party membership and the voting booths and segregated schools by color. It is the states that stopped an Edwards from migrating from dust-swept Oklahoma to California, punished an Uphouse for holding peace meetings in New Hampshire, and tried to punish a Swayze for teaching Marxist economics. It is states that tried to destroy the NAACP for refusing to make public its membership list, that denied a Gideon the right of counsel or a Brissel the right to give contraceptive information to patients. It is the federal courts, which in these and a hundred other similar cases, stepped in to vindicate the rights of individuals or organizations and associations against what appeared to be tyranny, and to enlarge those freedoms that were written into the Bill of Rights and the Fourteenth Amendment.

In the long run it will make very little difference which agency of the American people, state or national or, for that matter, corporate, conserves the land, ends pollution of the air and the waters, pays for education, provides for public health, cares for the aged and the infirm, improves the prisons and the penal codes, or revitalizes the cities. But it will make a fundamental difference if government at whatever level should venture to enter the areas traditionally closed to them, areas of speech, the press, association, religion, or if it should take refuge in its misdeeds in secrecy. The danger in our own day, as in Tocqueville's day, is that we blur the logic behind the limitation on governments and weakly acquiesce while government intervenes in those areas where it is forbidden to tread.

It is sobering that while for decades now presidents have called for a reduction in big government and a streamlining of big bureaucracy, none has been able to achieve these objectives, nor will they be able to do so in the future by rhetoric or by tinkering with administrative machinery. "When society requires to be rebuilt," wrote John Stuart Mill over a century ago, "there is no use attempting to rebuild it on the old plan. No great improvements in the lot of man are possible until a great change takes place in the fundamental constitution of our modes of thought."

However we may rail at big government and shudder at centralization, there will be no change in these institutions until we are prepared to challenge the assumptions upon which they are based. The initial assumption takes for granted traditional nationalism, a nationalism almost by its very nature self-centered, competitive, chauvinistic. That nationalism still seeks to solve problems that are by their very nature global, within the boundaries and with the mechanisms of individual nations. But traditional nationalism is as much of an anachronism in the world today and of tomorrow as was states' rights in the United States of 1860. All major problems now are global. They can be dealt with effectively only by international organizations and, if you will, by international bureaucracies. A recognition of this will doubtless call for additional bureaucratic supervision, but effective international regulation of problems that are global may contribute enormously both to the solution of those problems and to the reduction of bureaucratic duplication and of expenditures by a multitude of nations on those problems that are insoluble by individual nations. Consider, for example, and I cite merely a few, the impact of effective international control of nuclear armaments on both bureaucracy and on our finances, of atomic wastes and the destruction of life on the high seas, of the conservation of the resources of fossil fuel and the regulation of population. All of these matters carry with them not only enormous savings, savings both in administration and savings in the ultimate cost of these problems if they are not solved, but also savings even in administrative bureaucracy.

The security state also is a product not only of chauvinistic nationalism, but more particularly of those national rivalries and hostilities summed up in the term *Cold War*. The security system is not only our most expensive governmental activity, it is our most bureaucratic. I use the term *security system* rather than the term *military* because a security system involves so much more; it involves, of course, the CIA, the Atomic Energy Commission and its later incarnation, and all sorts of supporting organizations and supporting industries. It is our most bureaucratic and inevitably our most centralizing institution. If we could end the assumptions on which the Cold War was based—namely, that the world is irremediably divided into warring camps; that God and history have called upon the United States to represent one of these; that God and history somehow require that we should always be number one among the nations of the world (in a material sense, mind you, not a moral sense), and that they have placed on us responsibility to supervise the affairs of the rest of the world—if we could really, not just rhetorically, challenge these assumptions, we might bring about an even more drastic reduction in our own military establishment and in the establishments of rival nations than we have seen since the end of the Cold War. The impact of such a departure on the size and power of government and of bureaucracy and centralization is obvious.

Secrecy, traditionally the instrument of lawlessness and tyranny and abhorrent to the generation of the Founding Fathers, has now become an accepted and even legitimate instrument of American politics. Secret organizations like the CIA and others somewhat oddly lumped together under the term *intelligence community* (it is, I think, next to the term *athletic scholarship*, the most remarkable example of an oxymoron in our language) constitute, as we know, a vast bureaucracy with ramifications in almost every aspect of American life. Their activities are probably more highly centralized than those of any other branch of government except the military itself, of which they are, in a sense, an arm. By virtue of the cloak of secrecy that they wear, they represent more ostentatiously than any other precisely those dangers that Tocqueville envisioned.

Finally, I invoke a quotation from Tocqueville with which he began his discussion of the problem of centralization and liberty: everyone wants to be free; everyone wants to eat. In our own time the statement is merely symbolic, not literal. Everyone does indeed want to be free: free from bureaucratic controls, free from burdensome taxation, free to exercise and enlarge the area of private enterprise. Everyone does indeed want to eat: the poor want welfare, the aged want security, the ill and the handicapped want medical care, parents want education for their children, consumers want protection, environmentalists want to preserve natural resources, society at large wants to avoid pollution or disease or violence. The rich, too, want to be fed. They believe in private enterprise and delude themselves that corporations are somehow private rather than the product of very special privileges granted by the state and to be enforced by the state. When farmers are in trouble they invoke state aid. When cattlemen are in trouble they turn to the state. When coal miners are in trouble they recommend government takeover. When railroads and airlines are in trouble they persuade the government to subsidize them, at least the bankrupt ones. When shipping is in trouble it lives on government handouts. We have developed not only a welfare state with all of its bureaucracy for the poor, but a welfare state for corporations and business interests as well. Clearly the most completely socialized ingredient in our economy is not the poor who are on welfare, but the complex that President Eisenhower first publicly identified as the military-industrial, which we can now see embraces as well labor, banking, the scientific community, and the academy. If these want governmental protection and aid, as clearly they do, they must take for granted big government, big bureaucracy, and centralization.

Those who yearn to diminish the powers of government must learn to lower their expectations from government, to restrain their demands on nature, to temper their insistence on endless growth and progress that is almost entirely material. They must be prepared to abate their lust for world power, and temper that vanity which deludes them that they are called upon to preside over the future of mankind. They must be prepared to deal magnanimously with all peoples and nations and to deal justly and honestly with posterity. The Leviathan we must curb, the Behemoth we must bridle, is ourselves.

FOUR
The Military in a Democracy

As we have seen, Tocqueville predicted that centralization and bureaucracy would eventually subvert both liberty and democracy in America; he failed to perceive that government, even big government, could protect and enhance liberty as well as undermine it, and that the democratic processes could be and in fact were already being used to enlarge and realize democracy itself. But of the many forces making for centralization and at the same time threatening liberty, the most powerful by far had always been war, and it has been since that time. Tocqueville, of course, knew that. He knew that the American Revolutionary War had contributed enormously to a greater centralization of power in the American states, though not to the subversion of freedom, except perhaps the freedom of the Loyalists and perhaps, too, of the blacks who might have fared differently had Britain won. He was to live through the Napoleonic era, with its wars and its military preparations. He knew the impact of war and the military on freedom in the Old World.

Would war, would the military, endanger liberty and democracy in the New World? Tocqueville was sure that it would. "War does not always give over democratic communities to military government," he said,

> but it must invariably and immeasurably increase the powers of civil government; it must almost compulsorily concentrate

the direction of all men and the management of all things in the hands of the administration. If it lead not to despotism by sudden violence, it prepares men for it more gently by their habits. All those who seek to destroy the liberties of a democratic nation ought to know that war is the surest and shortest means to accomplish it. This is the first axiom of the science.

It was, above all, a protracted war that Tocqueville feared. Again, he had lived through the protracted French Revolutionary and Napoleonic wars, or knew them. "When a war has at length, by its long continuance," he wrote, "roused the whole community from their peaceful occupations and ruined their minor undertakings, the same passions which made them attach so much importance to the maintenance of peace will be turned to arms. War, after it has destroyed all modes of speculation, becomes itself the great and sole speculation, to which all the ardent and ambitious desires which equality engenders are exclusively directed."

And though Tocqueville could not possibly have foreseen the form that militarism would take in the era of the military-industrial complex, he did somehow apprehend that war would increasingly involve business and manufacturers and that inevitably the state and the interests that provided the materials for war would become mixed-up and interdependent. Thus, he said, in every kingdom a ruler will become the principal manufacturer. He collects and retains in his service a vast number of engineers, architects, mechanics, and handicraftsmen. He tends more and more to become the chief, or rather the master, of all other manufacturers.

Now the United States was born of war, her independence vindicated by war. Her symbols were and long remained military: Lexington, Concord, Bunker Hill, Valley Forge, Yorktown. Her earliest national songs, "Hail Columbia" and "The Star Spangled Banner," were born out of military crises and battles, and her heroes had earned their sanctification on the field of battle. Yet neither her soldiers nor her military leaders had ever posed a serious threat to the integrity of the Republic or to liberty. At the very threshold of independence, when all seemed to depend on the army, the Congress laid down the principle of subordination of the military to the civilian authority in all cases, and Washington scrupulously adhered to that principle. At the very end of the war, the president of the Congress would congratulate Washington that he had invariably regarded the rights of the civil power throughout the disasters and changes of the war, as indeed he had.

This experience should have encouraged Americans to take a more amiable view of the military, but it did not. So deep and inveterate was the distrust of everything military that it permeated the philosophical thought, the social conduct, and the legal arrangements that Americans made. It is a familiar story and I shall not enlarge upon it.

Let me give one example of each of these categories, of the philosophical, of the social, and of the legal. There is Benjamin Rush, famous Dr. Rush, one of the signers of the Declaration of Independence, who proposed that over the door of the War Department should be engraved, Office for the Butchering of the Human Race, Widow and Orphan-Making Office, Office for Creating Public and Private Vices, Office for Creating Poverty, Office for the Destruction of Liberty and National Happiness, and three or four more others of that kind. In the category of social attitude and conduct, consider the almost hysterical reaction of most Americans to the proposal to create the Society of the Cincinnati, a harmless organization. Some of the officers of the Revolution and their friends wanted to dangle a sword and wear a little ribbon. They had none of the designs on the treasury that, say, the Grand Army of the Republic or the American Legion had, or the Veterans of Foreign Wars. Nevertheless, the response to it was pretty much the response Senator McCarthy might have had, had he discovered communist cells at West Point or Annapolis—which he probably would have, had he got around to it. And for the legal and constitutional reaction, remember that almost every state constitution was established on the fundamental principle of the subordination of the military to the civilian. There is Massachusetts, which requires that "the military power shall always be held in exact subordination to her civil power and governed by it."

Tocqueville was familiar with most of this history, and he rejoiced in it. But here as so often his fears conquered his hopes. Surprisingly enough he thought that democracies would be more susceptible to military subversion than aristocracies. I shall not reproduce the whole of that fascinating passage, but sections of it: "Amongst aristocratic nations," he wrote, "the same inequality exists in the army as in the nation." The officer class was made up exclusively of aristocrats. Every French officer had to have sixteen quarterns, that is, four generations of nobility, before he could be an officer. Up until World War II the British army was officered entirely by the graduates of Sandhurst, and you had to be a very rich young man from a very famous family even to go to Sandhurst.

In Old World armies, privates had no possible scope for ambition. They were there as they were serfs on the land. But, Tocqueville pointed out, "in democratic armies all the soldiers may become officers, which makes the desire of promotion general, and immeasurably extends the bounds of military ambition. The officer almost always, on his part, sees nothing which naturally and necessarily stops him at one

grade more than at another; . . . his rank in society almost
always depends on his rank in the army." Thus, he wrote,
"his desire for advancement is ardent, tenacious, perpetual. . . . All the ambitious spirits of a democratic army are
consequently ardently desirous of war."

Well, that was not the way it had turned out in the United
States that Tocqueville knew. But there, too, he preferred the
conclusions of deductive logic to those of inductive facts. The
unsoundness of that deductive logic is, I think, familiar to all
who have any knowledge of most of nineteenth-century
American history. I shall not rehearse, as I had otherwise
planned to in a few swift lines, the history of admiration for
the military, but rather the subordination of the military to
the civilian. Jackson went to the White House straight from
New Orleans, as it were, and General Grant because he had
stood at Appomattox with its famous apple tree, and Mr.
Eisenhower after his claims while being made president of
Columbia University.

But the point is that Americans have continued to want a
military man but with civilian associations, as it were, who
is clearly subordinate to the civilian authority. They remained through the nineteenth and into the twentieth centuries faithful to the principle of the supremacy of the civil
authority far longer than Tocqueville had thought possible,
longer indeed than almost any disinterested observer would
have thought possible. When, fifty years after Tocqueville,
Bryce wrote his *American Commonwealth,* he did not think
it relevant to devote even one chapter out of a hundred and
nineteen to the military. When, after another half century,
and at a time when the United States was desperately
involved in the greatest war of her history, another perspicacious critic came to consider the American way of war, he
concluded: "The Americans wage war as they conducted

farming or business or the affairs of the kitchen, as an exercise in mechanics and business enterprise, with no hint of militarism in the Old World sense."

Clearly, the situation changed, changed profoundly and dramatically. And it is to the warnings and forebodings of a Tocqueville that we turn now, not to the indifference of a Bryce. The danger was not any crude threat of military usurpation. We feared neither a Caesar nor a Cromwell nor a Napoleon, and certainly not a Mussolini or a Hitler or a Stalin. What emerged was something dimly foreseen by Tocqueville but fundamentally new, the structure of a national security state, or as it was sometimes characterized, a weapons economy and a weapons state. It was more by far than the military-industrial complex against which President Eisenhower warned us in his farewell address. It was a military-industrial-financial-labor-academic-scientific aggre-gate, which exercised enormous political power as well as almost an independent economy, a self-sufficient society, and an alternative form of government.

How did all this come about in so short a time? Why did it develop, not in time of war, but in time of peace, or at least of technical peace? Why was it accepted with comparative equanimity by the vast majority of Americans? The national security state was a product of the Cold War, as the Cold War was in large measure the product of the psychology of the national security state. There has always been a bit of vindictiveness and even paranoia in our country after each of our wars, but in the past these were directed against those whom we had fought rather than against those with whom we were allied. That situation was for the first time reversed after the Second World War. We managed somehow not only to forgive, but also to help our defeated enemies, Japan and Germany and Italy. It was, astonishingly enough, the

Soviets we could not forgive. Doubtless that attitude was mutual.

It is not profitable here, I think, to enter into a consideration of the origins of the Cold War, a controversy that promises to persist as long as the controversy over the origins of the firing on Fort Sumter. Suffice it that the national security state, the weapons culture, the "economy of death" as it is sometimes called, did emerge out of and was part of the Cold War. The explanation for this situation is complex. We can distinguish only a few of the ingredients: a fear of communism, deeply rooted in both religious and secular convictions; a fear of the potentials of Soviet military might and of the threat that a victorious Soviet Union might pose to Central and Western Europe, that fear which found such eloquent and effective statement in Churchill's "Iron Curtain" speech in Fulton, Missouri; the transformation of war into a vast, intricately organized, scientific, technological enterprise; and, initially, the awesome power of a monopoly over the atomic weapon.

These considerations did not, I think, dictate the emergence of a national security state. They only provided the setting in which that state might flourish and come to maturity. After all, analogous circumstances had obtained after the First World War. Then, too, America bestrode the world like a colossus. Then, too, technology had made its profound impact. But then the United States dismantled its armed forces and retreated into isolation.

The most dramatic difference in American response to the postwar world in 1919 and 1945 was not, I think, in technology, but in ideology. That ideology, though it claimed plausible antecedents in American history, was fundamentally inconsistent with what had been the American faith or, if you will, the American creed. Where in the past that faith had been positive, confident, bold, imaginative, adventurous, and at times, magnanimous, the new ideology was negative, fearful, ingrown, churlish, parochial, and vindictive. It represented precisely what President Washington had warned against in his farewell address. "Nothing," wrote Washington,

> is more essential than that permanent, inveterate antipathies against particular nations and passionate attachments for others should be excluded, and that in place of them just and amicable feelings for all should be cultivated. The nation which indulges toward another an habitual hatred or an habitual fondness is in some degree a slave. It is a slave to its animosity or to its affection, either of which is sufficient to lead it astray from its duty and its interest. Hence, frequent collisions, obstinate, envenomed, and bloody contests, the nation prompted by ill will and resentment sometimes impels to war the government contrary to the best calculations of policy. The government sometimes participates in the national propensity and adopts through passion what reason would reject. In other times it makes the animosity of the nation subservient to projects of hostility instigated by pride, ambition, and other sinister and pernicious motives. The peace, sometimes even the liberty of nations, has been the victim.

So somewhat more obliquely said President Eisenhower in his farewell address: "This world must avoid becoming a community of dreadful fear and hate."

Cynics might allege that the disparate but mutually sympathetic forces that formed the national security complex—industry, business, finance, labor, politics, universities, the military, etc.—deliberately formulated an ideology sufficiently emotional and catholic in its appeal to assure widespread popular support, if not for the military at least for the security part of it, if not for war at least for a perpetual

preparation for war. They might find too a partial vindication in Tocqueville's prediction that in a democratic society
the military is ardent for war as the only means of advancement. They might find this by substituting for the formal
military all of those complex interests that have more to gain
from war, or from preparation for war, than they have from
peace. A more sobering analysis would, I think, conclude
that the ideological foundations of the Cold War were
already present in American psychology, and that the various elements in the national security complex were attracted
to that ideology as filings are attracted to a magnet.

It is unnecessary to elaborate upon the assumptions
behind the Cold War or behind the security-state psychology, that communism is a moral evil, that communism is
monolithic, that communism is committed to the subversion
and eventual destruction of all competing forms of government, that communism is militaristic and imperialistic, and,
conversely, that the American system, political and economic, represents morality and civilization, that it is the most
powerful nation on the globe, that we are responsible for
preserving democracy and freedom and enlightenment, that
we stand now in Armageddon in battle for the Lord, that in
this ultimate struggle between the forces of light and the
forces of darkness, those who are not for us are against us,
and that we are therefore justified in confounding their
politics and frustrating their knavish tricks (rather odd that
we should take over so readily the sentiments of the British
national anthem here), and that in order to achieve ultimate
victory we must always be number one militarily.

I do not assert that more than a minority of Americans
embraced the whole of this ideology, or that very many even
of the more paranoid still cling to it consciously. After all, we
have withdrawn our opposition to the admission of China

into the United Nations. We did make gestures called "détente" to both China and the Soviet Union. We did disband the House Un-American Activities Committee. We did even end the Vietnam War, or perhaps the Vietnamese ended it for us. Yet it is sobering that as yet there has been no formal or official repudiation of the assumptions behind Cold War psychology.

The Cold War, with all its far-reaching ramifications and consequences, was in large measure a product of a priori and deductive reasoning. Resort to such reason had been from the beginning alien to the American character and mind. John Dickinson's advice to his associates at the federal convention struck, I think, the right note: "Reason may mislead us. Experience must be our guide." By "reason" he meant, of course, rationalism. It was experience, not rationalism, that produced the Constitution. It was experience that guided the destiny of the new nation, whether under a Washington or an Adams or a Jefferson, all the same. It is experience that has, for the most part, presided over the conduct of American politics and American foreign affairs.

There is, of course, one major exception to this broad generalization, and it is one that should sober us; that is, the resort of the antebellum South to doctrinaire reasoning about the nature of the American constitutional system and about slavery, an attitude of mind and of psychology that permeated every aspect of southern life and, in the end, led the South down the road to war and destruction. Thus the doctrine of states' rights, which had had honorable antecedents, was perverted by southern statesmen like John C. Calhoun and Jefferson Davis to vindicate not liberty, as in Jefferson's Kentucky Resolutions, but slavery. In the process it became more and more attenuated, more and more out of touch with reality. In the end it arrived not only at the conclusion that as the states were sovereign and sovereignty was absolutely indivisible, the United States was not sovereign, but at the even more audacious conclusion that we find in Jefferson Davis's *Rise and Fall of the Confederate Government*, written twenty years after the war, that there was not, never had been, and never could be, such a thing as an American nation or an American people, only people of Mississippi, Alabama, Illinois, whatever you will, not Americans. Thus he rationalized the nation out of existence. Nothing in our own history, I think, so ominously reveals the consequences of doctrinaire reasoning as this chapter, this very important chapter, which tells how the South persuaded itself that slavery was a benign and civilizing institution, one worth a war, and that there was no nation called the United States.

In the antebellum South, slavery, to be sure, was fundamental and pervasive. It was a way of life, and the people are always under pressure to justify and vindicate their way of life, as we do today. It was no more limited to the economy than was our Cold War, or our present foreign policy, limited to the military. It embraced everything; it embraced slavery itself, of course, all of race relations, politics, law, education, religion, science, and morals. Turn where you will, there was the peculiar institution brooding over the whole southern landscape, the inner landscape as well as the outer landscape. To protect slavery and the way of life based upon it, the South closed ranks against the outer world, the outer world of freedom in the North and in Europe. To justify slavery, it relied upon religion, rewrote the Bible, rewrote ancient history, conjured up its own biology, created its own sociology and, with fateful consequences, its own interpretation of the very nature of the Constitution and of the Union. An attack upon slavery was an attack upon everything the South held most sacred, and those who attacked it were, of course, guilty of treason and of blasphemy.

The analogy between the proslavery philosophy and the national security philosophy of recent time is a close one. The South committed itself philosophically to the offense of slavery as its primary commitment. Just so the security state commits itself to security, always in military terms to be sure, as its primary commitment and responsibility. The Old South managed to hold together the most disparate elements—planters, businessmen, clergy, editors, intellectuals, nonslaveholding poor—all united in preserving a way of life, a way of slavery, just as the security state brought together its own elaborate and disparate complex that otherwise might be at each other's throats. Where by concentration on the one major issue of slavery the South glossed over and made innocuous those natural rivalries and hostilities that might otherwise have created controversy, discontent, and division, thus so the national security complex managed to hold together business and labor, Democrats and Republicans, the newspapers and the television media, the universities and the scientific community and the government in a single endeavor. The proslavery complex formulated an ideology both positive and negative. Positively, it celebrated slavery as benign, as an institution essential to the preservation of white supremacy and racial purity and true democracy and a high civilization. Negatively, it conjured up a national enemy who was also a moral enemy, namely the abolitionist North dedicated, as a leading southern newspaper indelicately observed in 1856, "to free niggers, free women, free land, free love, and Frémont." Just so, to defend slavery as a way of life and to defend the way of life resting on slavery, the South was prepared to silence all critics: to drive clergy from their pulpits, professors from their chairs, and editors from their newspapers; to censor literature, rifle the mails for subversive journals and pamphlets, and burn books; to withdraw into cultural and scientific isolationism. As that powerful editor DeBow put it in words that have a strangely contemporary ring,

> For us there has come to be but one sentiment. We deny the right of being called to account for our institutions, our policies, our laws and our government. For these there is no explanation to be made and no apology. It is sufficient that we, the people of half the states of this Union and our sovereign independents of all the people on earth, of all mortal men have decreed our institutions as they are and so will there to maintain them.

Something of this attitude dictated the reason and the policies of those who recently succumbed to obsessions about communist threats from without and communist subversion from within. They developed a fortress mentality as the South did. This mentality, in its zeal to protect our own form of government and our own way of life, denied the right of other people to do the same. It ignored in large measure the greatest revolution of history since the discovery of America, the emergence of two-thirds of the people of the globe out of colonialism and poverty and exploitation into the sun of modernity. It countenanced, too, the attempted subversion of our own constitutional system, the subversion of principles of separation of powers and of the subordination of the military to the civil authority, and the subversion of the guarantees of the Bill of Rights.

There is a final lesson to be drawn, I think, from the history of the Old South, a lesson, so far, rather than an analogy. Perhaps I should say a moral so far rather than an analogy. Defense of the Peculiar Institution against outside criticism and interference was inevitably transferred into offense. It was the South that seceded from the Union in order to preserve slavery, that organized an independent Confederate States. It was southern batteries that fired on Fort Sumter. It was the South that conducted the war. So, too, to defend our way of life we have found it necessary to wage a ten-year war against Vietnam, invade and destroy much of Laos and Cambodia, launch an invasion against Cuba, land twenty thousand marines in the Dominican Republic, and amass the most formidable arsenal of atomic weapons ever assembled. Creation of the security state was not a conspiracy, nor was the growth of a fortress mentality a product of paranoia. These developments are to be explained rather by the conjunction of a series of historical forces and pressures, the complex of powerful economic, scientific, and military interests that, in the absence of farsighted statesmanship and powerful countervailing pressures, developed a life of their own. Instead of yielding to the temptation to say that "passion's in the pot," we have been betrayed by what is false within.

Tocqueville saw intuitively what might occur if a military government or, let us say, a military-industrial complex were ever to develop in a democracy. He predicted that a sort of fusion would take place between the habits of official men and those in the military service. The administration would assume something of the military character and the army something of the usages of the civil administration. Clearly, in the past forty years, it is the administration rather than the military that has been responsible for creating the security state. It was President Truman who formulated the doctrine that led the United States to replace Britain in the Near and Middle East, and Truman, too, who made the decision to enter the Korean War. It was Eisenhower who sent warships and marines to Lebanon, Kennedy who launched the Bay of Pigs. Kennedy, too, was in part responsible for the initial ventures into Vietnam, which under the guiding and misguiding hands of presidents Johnson and Nixon escalated into a major war. The leading Cold War years came not from the military but from the civilian echelons of government: John Foster Dulles, Robert Lovett, James Forrestal, Dean Rusk, the Rostow brothers, McGeorge Bundy, and a host of others were recruited chiefly from the financial and legal communities, with aid and comfort from the universities. Clearly, none in the military and few in the industrial parts of the complex made contributions to the Cold War or to the security state. More significant are those contributions that we owe to such men as Senator Knowland, senators Goldwater and Stennis, Eastland, Thurmond, and Jackson, to name only a few examples, or to their associates in the other House who never even pretended to exercise oversight responsibilities over the CIA and the military, or Mendel Rivers of South Carolina, who boasted that he would pave South Carolina with so many military installations that it would sink into the sea. (He pretty well succeeded in that, too, by the way.)

I emphasize this because it illustrates so well the evaporation of those countervailing forces and the effective nullification of that separation of powers which the Founding Fathers believed would effectually restrain the military. That principle of countervailing forces has been built into our Constitution and our political system, and it has, until recently, dominated much of our social and economic systems as well. We balance states against the nation and the federal system. Two houses balance each other in every state legislature but that of Nebraska. Executive and legislative powers are a nice balance, and the judiciary independent.

Two major parties are awkwardly balanced, but as each represents a conglomeration of well-balanced interests, the balance works there as well. Religious freedom is preserved by balancing one hundred denominations and faiths against each other, and ethnic harmony is better preserved where there are a number of powerful ethnic groups, no one predominating.

The most serious danger spots in our society are to be found precisely where the principle of balance and the countervailing force does not flourish. It is against this background that we must interpret the sudden emergence of a complex that in large part nullified or paralyzed these traditional balances. What we had was not balance, but collaboration between what were designed to be counterbalancing forces, between the civil and the military, the executive and the Congress, business and labor. Industries no longer needed to compete for military contracts, they came for the asking, or even without being asked. Party opposition was silent, for opposition to the alleged needs of the military was looked upon as close to disloyalty. Congress is the watchdog of the treasury, but the military affairs committees of the two Houses rarely challenged any appropriations or expenditures. Indeed, they commonly gave the Pentagon more than it asked for. No wonder, since the committees were staffed almost wholly from the security complex. The Constitution of the United States, Article 1, Section 9, requires that a regular statement and account of the receipts and expenditures of all public monies shall be published from time to time. But in forty and more years there has never been an accounting, much less a public statement, of expenditures on the CIA, and when the Church and Pike reports hinted at the sums involved, Congress censored them and then voted $150,000 to find out who was responsible for leaking the information the committee had been set up to find and report on. Lewis Carroll himself could not have imagined anything more absurd than that episode.

Some advanced societies, such as Britain, Sweden, and Austria, have a bureaucracy that has security, ability, and prestige, and acts at least on occasions as an effective countervailing force to reckless or foolish politics. But just as presidents and congressmen enlisted in the national security complex, so too did administrative officials. Thus, the Bureau of the Budget should be independent, but it is not. Thus, the attorney general should enforce the Constitution and the law impartially, but he does not. Thus the CIA and the FBI, both affiliated with the Justice Department, should respect the Constitution, but they have not, certainly in the recent past. They, too, are essential elements in the military-security complex. How sobering it is that William Sullivan, one-time assistant director of the FBI, confessed to the Church committee that in all his experience with intelligence, an experience that countenanced a broad gamut of illegalities, he never once heard any question of legality raised. "We never gave a thought to this line of reasoning," he said, "because we were just naturally pragmatists," a definition of pragmatism which would have edified William James. Elsewhere, Mr. Sullivan testified that he never heard anyone question the legality or constitutionality of the campaign to discredit Dr. Martin Luther King.

As for subordinates in the federal administration, we know what has happened to those that blow the whistle on illegalities or corruption. President Carter promised to protect whistle-blowers. That is not quite what happened to District Attorney Marston of Philadelphia, or to the former CIA officer Mr. Snepp, who told the truth about the evacuation of Saigon. If the Justice Department allows itself to be enmeshed in the security complex, what is to be expected of other departments and bureaucracies more vulnerable to political pressure?

Nor do countervailing forces seem to work in the economy. Congressmen of both parties vied with each other to pass appropriations designed to bring war industries into their own districts, and with great astuteness the Defense Department planted military installations in somewhat more than three-fourths of all congressional districts. Efforts to close down useless military installations meets with as much opposition as efforts to close down dangerous nuclear plants or needless and unprofitable dams. Organized labor, which, in the past, was frequently critical of war, is won over by the promise of permanent employment for permanent security. No segment of our civilian economy was more enthusiastic in its support of the Vietnam War than labor. Only a handful of newspapers or journals are critical of military appropriations or military adventures, and television networks try to avoid controversy. Even the academic and scientific communities, traditionally symbols of independence, have been seduced and corrupted.

Years ago, Senator Fulbright, in one of his full-dress analyses of the workings of the military-industrial complex, charged that

> the adherence of the universities to the military involve the neglect and have carried far enough the betrayal of the university's fundamental reason for existence, which is the advancement of man's search for truth and happiness. It is for this purpose alone that universities receive and should receive the community's support. When the university turns away from its central purpose and makes itself an appendage to the government, concerning itself with techniques rather than ideals, dispensing conventional orthodoxy rather than new

ideas, it is not only failing to meet its responsibilities, it is betraying a public trust.

This betrayal was, in many respects, the most ominous feature of the emergence of the new security complex. It was the most ominous on a practical as well as on a moral ground. The purpose of freedom, including scientific and academic freedom, is, after all, a very practical one: to avoid error and discover truth. We know from the history of the Old South and the history of Nazi Germany the price a nation pays when it presides over distortion and betrayal of that principle of loyalty to truth. A government that exploits universities and scientific institutions because they are citadels of independent research will find that they no longer engage in independent research. "A state which dwarfs its scientists in order that they may be more docile instruments in its hands even for beneficial purposes," I am, of course, quoting John Stuart Mill, "will find that with small scientists no great thing can ever really be accomplished." Great institutions, from MIT on the East Coast to Berkeley on the West, engaged in secret research for military purposes during World War II, because they were persuaded that the survival of civilization itself was at stake. Perhaps it was. Once they had embarked upon this policy and program, however, they found that they were unable to extricate themselves from it when the war was over. World-famous institutions, and you can name a dozen of them, found themselves agents of government and increasingly dependent upon government largesse. More and more they discovered that their position was philosophically and often practically indefensible. It was indefensible philosophically because it repudiated in principle the unique position and responsibility that the university held; it was indefensible practically because it distorted the functions and the balance of the university itself.

The university is the one great global institution of the modern world. It antedated modern nationalism by some centuries. If it remains true to itself it shall outlive nationalism as we know it by some centuries. Its obligations and loyalties are not primarily to a particular society or economy or nation or to a particular generation but to all mankind, to posterity, to the search for truth. Because the university is an institution engaged in that search for truth, it must follow its own rules, its own instinct, and its own genius. It cannot be dictated to by secular authority if it is to survive. Independent research in any area can flourish only in an atmosphere of honesty and light. It cannot flourish in secrecy and darkness. To impose secrecy on the search for truth or on its publication is to frustrate the very function that the university is set up to perform.

All this was once familiar enough, so familiar it did not need to be restated. The generation that laid the foundation, not only for the American nation, but for American science and learning as well, took it all for granted. I shall not give you elaborate examples. Let me share with you, however, a passage from Jefferson's letter to his friend Rittenhouse, familiar perhaps to some of you. Jefferson had given up all of his darling occupations of scholarship and learning and farming to be governor of Virginia during the war, and Rittenhouse, next to Franklin the greatest scientist of his day in America, had also given up his scientific pursuits to be secretary of the state of Pennsylvania. In 1778, Jefferson wrote him:

> Your time for two years past has, I believe, been practically employed in the civil government of your country. Though I have been aware of the authority our cause would acquire that

from its being known that yourself and Dr. Franklin were
zealous friends to it and I am myself impressed with the sense
of arduousness of government and the obligation those are
under who are able to conduct it, yet I am also satisfied that
there is an order of genius above that obligation and therefore
exempt from it. Nobody can conceive that nature ever intended
to throw away a Newton upon the occupations of a crown. It
would have been a prodigality from which even the conduct of
Providence might have been arraigned had he been by birth the
next to what was so far below him.

Perhaps Dr. Edward Jenner of smallpox fame put it more
succinctly: "The sciences are never at war. Peace must always
preside in those bosoms whose object is the augmentation of
human happiness."

The security state as it has operated in the United States in
recent years corrupted not only politics and the economy, it
corrupted morals as well. In the eyes of its manipulators and,
presumably, its beneficiaries, it justified violation of international law, as in the invasion of Cambodia; violations of the
laws of war of the Geneva Convention, as in the use of
napalm and in the indiscriminate bombing of villages;
assassination, as in the Phoenix program (rather a nice irony
to give it that name, by the way—after all, the phoenix was
the classical emissary of peace) or the attempts to assassinate
heads of state whose conduct we disapproved of. It justified
lying and deception at home and abroad: the deception of
Tonkin Bay, which of course was fraudulent; those absurd
body counts, which in the end eliminated on paper almost
the whole adult male population of North Vietnam; perjury
before congressional committees; the use of that Old World
hated device—provocative agents. It encouraged wholesale
violation of the Constitution and the Bill of Rights, requiring
a secrecy that undermined the very foundations of democ-

racy by denying people the opportunity to know what their government was doing, and providing a cloak for chicanery, lawlessness, and treachery. It justified a double standard of morality in international and in national relations. Imagine applying to our highest officers in the Vietnam War the standards we established in the Nuremberg and Tokyo war crime trials. It seduced honorable men into dishonorable conduct, and moral men into justifying immorality. Thus an honorable man like Robert McNamara could bring himself to say that "the greatest contribution Vietnam is making, right or wrong is beside the point, is that it is developing an ability in the United States to fight a limited war, to go to war without the necessity of arousing public ire. In that sense, Vietnam is a necessity in our history because this is the kind of war we will be likely to be facing in the next fifty years." Think of the consolation it must be for the Vietnamese to reflect that the seven million tons of bombs dropped on them added to our education. Thus could another honorable man, Senator Symington of Missouri, one-time secretary of the Air Force, assure Congress that "the destruction of civilians is an unavoidable result of modern total war. The opinion that war is immoral is a fallacy, or a recent one, for anybody in the military establishment. I wonder how and why it ever came up." And the CIA director, Richard Helms, as you know, won national applause when he justified violation of the Constitution and of international law on the plea that his first loyalty was to a higher law, that of the CIA.

The fundamental and irremediable flaw in the concept of the security state is of course the concept of security itself. First, last, and all the time the term *security,* as used by its sponsors and managers, means military security. More than three centuries ago, Francis Bacon wrote that "walled towers, ordnance, stored arsenals and armor, goodly races of chariots of war, elephants, artillery, and the like—all this is but a sheep in a lion's skin except the breed and disposition of the people be stout."

Security is not an end in itself. It is the means to an end. It makes all the difference, after all, what it is that we secure. The only use of the word *secure* in the Constitution of the United States is the dedication in the preamble, "and secure the blessings of liberty to ourselves and our posterity." Nor is security to be found in military might. There was no security in Hitler's Germany, not even for the German people, not certainly for that civilization Germany had developed over the centuries, nor in the end for the nation itself. There was doubtless security of a sort in the former Soviet Union, but it was not a security that we would ever desire. Security can be found in the end only in the wisdom, the intelligence, the courage, and the virtue of a people. It is not to be confused with power, just the point President Kennedy made in one of the last and perhaps the most moving of his speeches, that our country should "match its military strength with moral strength, its wealth with wisdom, and its power with purpose." That was an echo ringing down the centuries of the noble words of Pericles that happiness was not to be found in power or in wealth or in security, but that the "secret of happiness is freedom and the secret of freedom a brave heart."

FIVE

Political Equality and Economic Inequality

   The grand theme of *Democracy in America* is the reconciliation of equality or democracy—for he used the words interchangeably—with liberty. Democracy, he was confident, was the wave of the future (he was not really all that confident, but he insisted in the book that he was). Democracy had triumphed in America; its triumph in the Old World was well nigh inevitable. The prospect of that triumph was both exhilarating and sobering: exhilarating because democracy made for justice, sobering because it threatened liberty, which was, after all, the greatest and the ultimate end of government.

   I have already examined some of the threats that Tocqueville saw, either explicit or implicit, in democracy—the malaise of mediocrity, the tyranny of the majority, the danger of bureaucratic centralization to liberty, and the menace of military subversion. These perils were conjured up on the whole by deductive reasoning, not by examples or by evidence, and they did not in fact materialize during the nineteenth century. But we may not therefore conclude that they can be dismissed, for they did in fact materialize in that Old World which most deeply concerned Tocqueville, and they loom ominously over the American scene today and tomorrow. Clearly, Tocqueville was prophetic in the warnings he addressed to the nations of Europe. It is possible that he may prove justified, more than a century later, in the warnings he addressed to the American people.

I turn now to a consideration of that paradox which Tocqueville himself thought most arresting, the paradox of an ardent passion for equality married to an equally ardent passion for individualism; the threat of what we would now call class conflict, which, though it might achieve a greater degree of both equality and justice, might at the same time destroy liberty. These fears, as we have seen, were rooted in Tocqueville's perception that given a choice, a democratic people will inevitably prefer equality to liberty. "It has been said a hundred times," he reminds us, "that our contemporaries are far more ardently and tenaciously attached to equality than to freedom," and he proceeded to explain that while democratic communities have a natural taste for freedom, for equality their passion "is ardent, insatiable, incessant, invincible: they call for equality in freedom; and if they cannot obtain that, they still call for equality in slavery. They will endure poverty, servitude, barbarism—but they will not endure aristocracy." And he predicted that all men and all powers seeking to cope with this irresistible passion will be overthrown and destroyed. Freedom cannot be established without it, and despotism itself cannot reign without its support.

Elsewhere, Tocqueville sounded a more foreboding note. The American environment, he asserted, made possible both equality and inequality. If the forces making for inequality triumphed, the consequences would be disastrous. "If ever the free institutions of America are destroyed, that event may be attributed to the omnipotence of the majority, which at some future time urge the minority to desperation and oblige them to have recourse to physical force. Anarchy will then be the result."

It was not black slaves he had in mind, but a pseudoaristocracy of the rich, whose ambitions might threaten the principle of equality. He called this, for want of a better name, a "manufacturing aristocracy." It was new and it was ominous, without tradition and without a sense of fiduciary obligation either toward working men or toward society or posterity. It did not even form a class, as had the landed aristocracy of the Old World, but was merely an agglomeration of individuals. Where the territorial aristocrats of an earlier time were bound by law and by usage to come to the relief of their serving men, as Tocqueville put it, "the manufacturing aristocracy of our age first impoverishes and debases the men who serve it, and then abandons them to be supported by the charity of the public." No wonder, he concluded, "that the manufacturing aristocracy which is growing up under our eyes is one of the harshest which ever existed in the world, . . . if ever a permanent inequality of conditions and aristocracy again penetrate into the world, it may be predicted that this is the channel by which they will enter."

Let us consider this most intractable of the paradoxes that American democracy presented to the mind of the philosopher, the fact that while almost everything in the New World favored both equality and individualism, the two were logically and, as it proved, historically incompatible. The paradox of the dedication to freedom and the commitment to slavery was, to be sure, more ostentatious than that of equality and individualism, but it was in a sense an artificial paradox. It was a product not of nature but of man. When Jefferson said all men are created equal, he was speaking not only for hope but also for what he thought was a scientific fact at the moment of birth. In the eyes of nature, they were equal; nature did not know any difference between white and black, male and female, rich and poor, or any other. All of these differences were the products of society, not of nature. Slavery was in that sense artificial, a product not of nature but of men. It could be resolved, though at an inordinate cost, without violating the laws of nature, and it was eventually so resolved. But individualism, like equality, was rooted in nature, and in addition, it was nourished by history, favored by law, and vindicated by results.

It is interesting in this connection to note that the word *equality* is not to be found in the Constitution of the United States as it came from the hands of the Framers. It appears for the first time in the Fourteenth Amendment of 1868: "nor shall any State . . . deny to any person within its jurisdiction the equal protection of the laws."

For almost a century, that clause of the Constitution was deliberately ignored; indeed, worse than ignored, it was repudiated, and when in 1954 it did emerge, it was largely confined to the areas of social and political equality, thus the right to an equal education, thus the equal right to vote, etc. It was not extended into the economic arena. Indeed, we have yet to read a substantive meaning of equal protection into the realm of economy. Neither the court nor the Congress is at this stage prepared to say that equal protection of the laws means an equal right to a job, means equality in housing, means equality in medical care, means equality in prison and penal conditions, means equality in all those nonpolitical, nonlegal, and we might say, nonsocial areas. Thus a century after we got rid of the paradox of freedom and slavery, the paradox of equality and individualism persists and may indeed be getting more aggravated.

Let us turn then to a consideration of individualism, a word, let it be noted, that Tocqueville himself coined and used for the first time in *Democracy in America*. We have seen that the environment, what the Enlightenment called "climate," of the New World, as well as the circumstances of its settlement, favored, if it did not indeed dictate, social equality. It favored with equal impartiality individualism and equality, yet from the beginning there was a latent incompatibility between the two qualities. For equality meant, or at least implied, a leveling down; it meant equality before the law, equality in political rights, equality of opportunity. Everyone would be in the same boat. But individualism, which required just as sharp a break from the Old World institutions and habits as equality, had emphasized not similarities but differences, not uniformity but extremes. The class society of the Old World dictated marked differences between classes but very few differences within any one class. The classless society of the New World imposed something like uniformity in social and public life but permitted, indeed encouraged, individual initiative to achieve distinction in other areas, especially in the economic and in the intellectual. Indeed, it made this distinction an insignia for a new kind of class, not a legal class, but a real class economically.

Individualism was as deeply rooted in American enterprise as equality. Everything seemed to encourage it: the "sifted seed" theory of immigration; the necessity that the New World presented for talent and industry and resourcefulness in order to survive; the recognition of talent for leadership in a society that was not hierarchical and had impartial rewards to ability or industry wherever they appeared, and had provisions even for luck; the religious freedom, which did not permit an established church, but permitted each to go to such heaven as he imagined his own way, or even to refuse; the abundance of land to be cultivated, of resources to be exploited by those who were enterprising; the reliance on individual initiative for survival; the educational enterprise, which permitted those who were clever to go as far as they would; the easy access to professions, to the military, to public office; and the invitation to speculation, which put a premium on cleverness and cunning. Those of this generation, surrounded by regulations and requirements of all kinds, have sometimes failed to realize how casual these matters were in Tocqueville's day. There was no problem with admission to the bar or to the practice of medicine. You hung out a shingle and decided law was not a good profession, so became a doctor. (In Indiana, for example, all that was required in the long part of the nineteenth century was the signatures of two lawyers that you were a man of good character and you were able to practice law. I must say it was not as easy as one might suppose—it is not always easy to find two people who will testify to a lawyer's good character. In Ohio, until passage of the state's Medical Practice Act of 1896, anyone could be a doctor who registered at the nearest probate court.)

The law, too, favored individualism. The emphasis upon individual rights and liberties, the encouragement in the absence of public activities of private enterprise, the broad scope given newly emergent corporations, the encouragement to speculation, the absence of effective governmental controls or regulations, the protection of migration from state to state, the ease of entry into business—all of these encouraged adventure and enterprise. Underlying all these was an awareness of almost limitless natural resources eagerly awaiting exploitation, and the concept of infinity that for so long dominated American thought. Indeed, one of the great crises of our time is that at last we have to adjust to the fact of finite resources, we who for three hundred years took for granted that our resources were infinite. So deeply ingrained were these notions and so powerful the commitment to individualism that when in the post–Civil War years the task of building railroads, irrigating lands, harvesting forests, exploiting coal and iron and oil and precious metals proved beyond the resources of individuals, the government itself was enlisted in the enterprise, but not as a prime mover and beneficiary, only as a collaborator, and it was persuaded to create a welfare state not for the poor but for corporations. All this anticipated by almost a century the analogous creation of that military-industrial-financial-labor-academic-scientific complex which was the subject of my last chapter.

Tocqueville himself used the term *individualism* almost in a pejorative sense, for he feared that individualism, unless controlled or modified by other forces, would be fatal to the well-being of society. "Individualism," he wrote, "at first, only saps the virtues of public life; but, in the long run it attacks and destroys all others, and is at length absorbed in downright egotism. Egotism is a vice as old as the world, which does not belong to one form of society more than to another: individualism is of democratic origin and threatens to spread in the same ratio as the equality of conditions." And Tocqueville saw too the explanation of this, that democracy had already broken the "cake of custom," that a democratic society lacked those traditions and institutions whose business it was to preserve old habits and practices and all possessions as well. He saw, too, that in democratic nations the "woof of time is every instant broken, and the track of generations effaced. Those who went before are soon forgotten; of those who will come after no one has any idea. . . . Thus not only does democracy make every man forget his ancestors, but it hides his descendants, and separates his contemporaries from him; it throws him back forever upon himself alone, and threatens in the end to confine him entirely within the solitude of his own heart." A generation later, Henry James was to make this perception the theme of a score of his novels, nowhere more pointedly than in the one aptly named *The American*, which is indeed a fascinating study of the inability of Americans to break through the "cake of custom," the centuries of tradition to which French aristocracy paid allegiance.

Tocqueville himself thought, or hoped, that the atomizing effect of individualism and competitiveness on the American society might be counterbalanced by the voluntary private association. This was at the time, and long remained, a valid expectation. The voluntary association was a contribution as distinctive to and as important to American democracy as the principle of limited government. In forming the American Union and in molding the American character, it played a decisive role. Eventually, it was to perform a large portion of those duties elsewhere performed by government itself. You may remember Tocqueville's famous observation that whatever is ordinarily done in France by the government and in England by members of the aristocracy is done in America by ordinary men and women banding together to do it. Ultimately, the voluntary private association was indeed to be itself a form of government, as the American Bar Association is a form of government, as labor unions are a form of government. Union members prefer to pay allegiance to union decisions rather than to decisions of the president or of the Congress. Most of the major institutions of society and politics in Tocqueville's day, after all, were voluntary; thus the churches, the embryonic labor unions, political parties, academies and colleges, farmers' unions, professional organizations, reform associations, and scores of others, including even the militia. Together, they probably performed more and more valuable services than those performed by the formal government. These, as Tocqueville wrote, led a great many citizens to value the affection of their neighbors, perpetually bringing them together and forcing them to help one another in spite of propensities that might have severed them.

Yet almost from the beginning individualism and the spirit of competition triumphed over communitarianism and the spirit of cooperation. How indeed could it be otherwise in a society that was wide open, in an economy that constantly invited exploitation, in a political system that rewarded enterprise? Of what use was competition in a class society like that of the French or the English, where advancement and wealth were open only to those who could submit the proper social and cultural credentials and where, for that matter, the status of almost everyone was irremediably fixed at birth? But in Tocqueville's day, the American was the most competitive of societies. Nothing was really fixed by class. Competition knew or acknowledged no class barriers. Classes in America might mean something to those who thought they belonged to them, but they meant nothing to the people at large. Thus an Adams was an aristocrat, if there were aristocrats, and an Andrew Jackson an upstart, but in 1829 it was Jackson who was in the White House, not John Quincy Adams. It was the French-born Stephen Gerard and the German-born John Jacob Astor who were the two richest men in America. Even in Tocqueville's day, you could not conceivably have that in any Old World country.

By the time Tocqueville published the second volume of his *Democracy in America* in 1840, almost all white Americans, at least in the North, had achieved a rough social equality and, if male, political equality as well. Economically, American society was certainly more nearly egalitarian than any to be found in Europe. But especially with the burgeoning of the new immigration from Ireland and then Scandinavia and Germany, inequalities in wealth were beginning to be ostentatious, and these carried over to some extent in the social arena. The industrial revolution that flourished during and after the Civil War, the building of the railroad network, the rise of modern corporations and trusts and monopolies, the discovery and exploitation of precious metals and iron in the West and of oil in Pennsylvania and elsewhere, the rapid growth of cities and with them of ghettos and slums—all these produced economic equalities and dramatized economic inequalities. As early as 1879, Henry George could dramatize the contrast between progress and poverty. In 1890, the immigrant Jacob Riis could describe how the other half lived. A few years later, Henry Demarest Lloyd saw the American economy in terms of wealth against commonwealth. At that time, even the amiable William Dean Howells, born in Tocqueville's day, could describe society in poetic terms that would have been meaningless to a Jefferson: "I looked and saw a splendid pageantry of beautiful women and of lordly men taking their pleasure on a flowery plain where poppies and the red anemone flickered about their feet. I looked again and saw that flowery space stirring as if alive beneath the tread that rested now upon an old man's head and now upon a baby's gasping face or mother's bosom, and what would seem the red of flowers was blood." That, coming from a man who tried to portray the more amicable features of American life, as he himself said, is something of an indication of the realization of what was happening in America by its most astute students. In 1888, James Bryce could warn Americans that they were developing greater extremes of wealth and poverty than could be found even in England; and the chief justice of Wisconsin asserted at the same time even more dramatically that "the accumulation of individual wealth seems to be greater than it ever has been since the downfall of the Roman Empire, and for the first time in our history money is taking the field as an organized power."

Even on the somewhat slender basis of his American experience, at a time when economic inequalities were still meager, Tocqueville had predicted that the omnipotence of the majority might drive powerful minorities to desperation and oblige them to have recourse to force and violence. Fifteen years later, chastened by his own experience in the coup d'état in France of 1848 (and remember he was forced out of the Ministry of Foreign Affairs at that time), Tocqueville saw the danger coming rather from frustrated or outraged majorities than from minorities, but it was still the same danger. "The revolution of 1848," he wrote in his *Recollection,*

> should not have surprised the world as much as it did. Had no one noticed that for a long time the people had been continually gaining ground and improving their condition, and that their importance, education, desires and power were all constantly growing? Their prosperity had also increased, but not so fast, and it was getting close to that limit which, in old societies, cannot be passed. . . . How could it have failed to occur to the poorer classes, who were inferior but nonetheless powerful, that they might use their power to escape from their poverty and inferiority? For sixty years they had been working towards this end. At first the people hoped to help themselves by changing the political institutions, but after each change they found that their lot was not bettered, or that it had not improved fast enough to keep pace with their headlong desires.

Just what we seem to be fighting in our country with every change of administration and every new program. The situation is more alike than it is different. "Inevitably," Tocqueville wrote, they were bound to discover sooner or later that what held them back in their place was not the constitution of the government, but the unalterable laws that constitute society itself; and it was natural for them to ask whether they did not have the power and the right to change these too. . . . And to speak specifically about property, . . . when all the privileges that cover and conceal the privilege of property had been abolished and property remained as the main obstacle to equality among men and seemed to be the only sign thereof, was it not inevitable . . . that the idea of abolishing it should strike minds that had no part in its enjoyment? . . .

Will socialism remain buried in the contempt that so justly covers the socialists of 1848? I ask the question without answering it. I am sure that in the long run the constituent laws of our modern society will be drastically modified. . . . But will they ever be abolished and replaced by others?

Laws were indeed to be not only modified, but abolished, and in part at least, by those teachings that had already sounded when Tocqueville wrote, for this observation came just two years after the publication of Karl Marx's *Communist Manifesto*. The prophecy so farsighted was to be fulfilled in the Old World, not in the New. We in the United States take that for granted because we think of the redistribution of property and revolution almost wholly in terms of violence, not in terms of law. But Americans did not need to resort to violence to have a revolution. The American constitutional system was itself revolutionary, as indeed the whole principle of popular sovereignty and of majority rule was revolutionary. In the century after Tocqueville wrote, the American people did use their Constitution and laws to enlarge both political and social equality: the Thirteenth Amendment, which freed the slaves; the Fourteenth and the Fifteenth, which were designed to confer on freedmen full political and social equality; later, the women's suffrage amendments; a large body of civil rights legislation; and alongside these, a substantial body of judicial decisions that both protected and expanded minority rights.

How does it happen that the American people did not use the Constitution or the laws to achieve a greater economic equality? How does it happen that Tocqueville's prediction was not fulfilled in the United States? Certainly the potentialities for legal revolution were and still are there. It would take me too far astray to elaborate on these. It is sufficient to call a few of them to attention very briefly. As I noted earlier, our Constitution is a revolutionary document, and Tocqueville was profound in his insight that we could have our revolution without having a revolution. We could have a legal revolution.

Three examples will suffice. There is first the tax power, far and away the most revolutionary power lodged in government. Elsewhere in the Western world the tax power has been the instrument for the control and subsequently for the redistribution of wealth. How did it happen that it has never been effectively used for this purpose in the United States, or even in individual states exercising their power to experiment within the federal system? After tremendous struggle, the power to tax incomes was finally, in 1913, granted the federal government by the Sixteenth Amendment. No more obvious or elementary method of redistributing wealth than this has ever been devised, yet this has never been used for that purpose. When, during the Second World War, President Roosevelt rather casually suggested that the government tax away all incomes over the then high level of $25,000, a cry of outrage went up among the property classes, and there was no sound of approval from the poor. Certainly, taxation has not changed the familiar pattern of American wealth as it has changed the pattern of wealth in Britain or the Scandinavian countries or the Low Countries and elsewhere on the globe.

The second constitutional and legal method of achieving a revolutionary redistribution of wealth is that which found approval from that revolutionary radical Alexander Hamilton, and which again is taken pretty much for granted in most Old World countries and, as far as I know, in almost all Third World nations: the nationalization of natural resources. There is, I know, the problem of just compensation in our constitutional system, a pretty formidable requirement. But the student of national character must ask why the government did not assert title to oil and metals and public lands at the very outset, as Hamilton said it should. Why did it not itself build the railroads as, after all, it builds highways today, or create national airlines, or establish public radio and television as almost every government in the rest of the world does? But we have not done so. Indeed, the idea is so alien to us that I suppose nine out of ten Americans cannot imagine anything but commercial radio and television. (After all, what have they got to listen to or look at but the advertisements on most of it?)

A third method of achieving equality of economic and other opportunities is implicit, and in the eyes of some jurisprudents explicit, in that equal protection of the laws clause to which I have referred earlier. That clause was invoked to require equality in schooling, *Brown v. Board of Education;* equality in voting, *Baker v. Carr;* equality in many areas of legal rights for the wards of states, women, etc., such as the Miranda decision or the abortion decision. But again it has been applied almost wholly in the social or the political or the legal-technical areas, not in the economic.

Why have courts been so reluctant to extend their guarantees to the realm of economic opportunity? Why has public opinion been so reluctant to demand legislation that would clarify or require extension into these areas? Why, in short, has American democracy, that democracy which Tocqueville predicted would sweep the Western world and revolutionize it, been deeply conservative, when democracy in the Old World and wherever it has been allowed to function in other parts of the globe, has been on the whole radical and revolutionary?

The explanation in Tocquevillian terms can be found, I think, in the interaction between those two forces that he himself thought the most powerful: majority rule and individualism. He was fearful that majoritarianism would take over the surrender to its natural propensity for tyranny with catastrophic consequences. In that event, it was not the majority that imposed its will on desperate minorities, but the spirit of individualism and private enterprise that permeated majorities and persuaded or seduced them into supporting even the most extreme manifestations of private enterprise. The danger today is no more from majority tyranny than it was in the 1830s when Tocqueville first sounded the alarm. It is rather in that excess of the virtue of individualism that we now call private enterprise, but which is no longer private but public, and which, for that matter, is no longer very enterprising. The operation of the military-industrial-financial-labor-academic-scientific complex is an example of this. This group or complex does not constitute a majority, but it appears to represent a majority. And to speak for it, it does not formally exercise what we call tyranny, and as for all its triumphs and conquests, these have been brought about by legal means and are not therefore tyrannical. But its character and conduct takes on more and more the character of tyranny. In all this, Tocqueville's fears may yet be vindicated.

Certainly there is no tyranny; whatever is done is done under the Constitution. Certainly there is no overt flouting of majority will; those who carried through the revolution of the last decades have done so with the support of the people, sometimes massive support. Certainly, too, there is no conspiracy, though there have been conspirators; and though there is a tendency to resort to secrecy, on the whole programs have been openly acknowledged and debated. Nor do we have even an imitation or an echo of those class conflicts of which Tocqueville himself was so sharply aware and which Marx had already predicted. An American proletariat has not sought to impose its will on a bourgeoisie, for we do not have in America a proletariat or a bourgeoisie any more than we have a peasantry, an aristocracy, a military class, an ecclesiastical class, or even an intelligentsia. But we are uncomfortably aware that whatever the ingredients in the military-industrial mix, and whatever the processes, the consequences are not far from those that Tocqueville predicted.

Tocqueville asserted resoundingly that the triumph of democracy was inevitable. Yet he was not really as certain of this as he sounded, even in the *Democracy*. He noted that the great empire of Russia might someday dominate Europe and the world, though he did not see the form that dominion would take. He was not certain that democracy might not itself succumb to the tyranny of the majority, to centralization, to the power of the military, or to other excesses. He hoped, but he was not confident, that the Americans, inspired by public philosophy, blessed by the richest resources ever vouchsafed a people, enlightened by laws and by education, would be able to continue along the roads that they were traveling. Yet he predicted, as we recall, that the Union would not hold as long as slavery threatened it, and he feared other dangers almost as grave as those of slavery. He believed that democracy would conquer Europe, that democracy was indeed the wave of the future, yet here, too, he was chastened by experience, even in his own lifetime. For he came later to the study of the ancien régime, and that, plus his own experience in government and in the coups d'état of Napoleon I and Napoleon III, brought home to him the sobering fact that ruling classes did not learn from experience, and that a people is easily seduced, as the French people had been seduced by the first and third Napoleons.

The basic question of the future of democracy is, of course, very much with us. It is indeed in some respects more urgent than it was when Tocqueville wrote, for its future is more uncertain than it was one hundred and fifty years ago. Is our kind of democracy or equality still valid? Can it survive in the world of today and in the future, if any? Clearly, an American democracy does not now seem to be the wave of the future, not at least in its American form. Are perhaps all nation-states outmoded? Must we not take to mind and to heart here the sagacious admonition of Tocqueville, stated best in his *Recollections*: "The more I study the former state of the world, . . .when I consider the prodigious diversity found there, . . . I am tempted to the belief that what are called necessary institutions are only institutions to which one is accustomed." We might take some counsel from that admonition. And we can take some counsel, I think, from the concluding page of his *Democracy in America*:

> I am full of apprehensions and of hopes. I perceive mighty dangers which it is possible to ward off—mighty evils which may be avoided or alleviated; and I cling with a firmer hold to the belief, that for democratic nations to be virtuous and prosperous they require but to will it. I am aware that many of

my contemporaries maintain that nations are never their own masters here below, and that they necessarily obey some insurmountable and unintelligent power, arising from anterior events, from their race, or from the soil and climate of their country. Such principles are false and cowardly; such principles can never produce aught but feeble men and pusillanimous nations. Providence has not created mankind entirely independent or entirely free. It is true that around every man a fatal circle is traced, beyond which he cannot pass; but within the wide verge of that circle he is powerful and free: as it is with man, so with communities. The nations of our time cannot prevent the conditions of men from becoming equal; but it depends upon themselves whether the principle of equality is to lead them to servitude or freedom, to knowledge or barbarism, to prosperity or wretchedness.

SIX

The Agenda of the 1990s

The subject of the previous chapters is Tocqueville's application to later developments in America; in a sense, a discussion of the agenda of the 1990s and beyond may be considered an appendix to this topic. I am still considering many of the same issues that Tocqueville considered, looking forward, as Tocqueville himself looked forward, to some of the problems that confront us and will confront the next generation. And I begin, in fact, with a quotation from Tocqueville, who is, as you know, endlessly quotable: "The society of the modern world," he wrote in 1840,

> has but just come into existence. Time has not yet shaped it into perfect form: the great revolution by which it has been created is not yet over: and amid the occurrences of our time it is almost impossible to discern what will pass away with the revolution itself, and what will survive its close. The world which is rising into existence is still half encumbered by the remains of the world which is waning into decay; and amidst the vast perplexity of human affairs, none can say how much of ancient institutions and former manners will remain, or how much will completely disappear.

That is as true today as when he wrote it.

The crisis so recently posed by the threat of the use and abuse of nuclear power, the present-day crisis of the depletion of "energy" (a term which is a kind of euphemism, of course, for those natural resources upon which we have relied)—both are symptom and symbol of that complex of crises which are so importunately on the agenda of the 1990s and of succeeding decades. These crises are not local or national, they are global. They mark and dramatize what is perhaps the greatest watershed of modern history.

There have been three or four of these historical watersheds. The first, that which we associate with the Renaissance, ushered in the modern age. It shattered the accepted view of the world—accepted, that is, in the West—by introducing a new world of man and a new world of nature, and it shattered the unity imposed upon the West by the Catholic church by the rise of Protestantism and of secularism.

The second great watershed came with the introduction of modern science, which we associate with Newton and the Newtonian age and the spread of the Enlightenment, whose distinguishing feature was the substitution of nature for God and of reason for faith. No less shattering was the emergence with the American and French revolutions of modern nationalism, which, for better or worse, and clearly a mixture of both, has dominated the historical scene for some two hundred years.

The third watershed—these come now with increasing frequency—was associated with the Darwinian revolution and its limitless implications for the substitution of a dynamic and organic universe for one that had been supposed to have been static and unalterable, an order whose destinies might be controlled by man rather than by God or by impersonal cosmic forces, and with this the development of a nationalism that accommodated itself increasingly to the law of the survival of the fittest rather than to the precepts of the Enlightenment: that is, a nationalism that was Darwinian rather than Newtonian.

The current watershed is the most convulsive and probably the most ominous of all. Now, for the first time, those rivers that pour down may inundate us and put an end to history itself. That could not be said or even suspected of any of the previous watersheds. I can only sketch the lineaments of the new world that has burst upon us with such spectacular rapidity, and I can only suggest those prodigious problems that glare upon us from every quarter of the horizon. With most of these you are indeed familiar: population, which promises to reach seven billion in the lifetime of young people today; the exhaustion of the basic resources of energy, such as oil and gas; the erosion of productive land, the amount of which is decreasing every year as population is increasing; the pollution of air and water, which threatens man, animals, and crops; the inability to control the use and abuse of outer space or even the belligerent control of the weather; the almost systematic destruction of oceans, with its far-reaching impact on food supplies and on the balance of nature; violence and terrorism, which defy reason as they defy control; the recent militarization of almost everything from politics and society to science and learning; and, brooding over all of these, the threat (until the collapse of the Soviet Union) of nuclear war or of plutonium poisoning and the concentration of national and world resources, intellectual and scientific as well as material, on preparation for war, and along with this the breakdown of international law and the signal inability of international law or international organizations to control, much less dissipate, all of these threats. Nor has the threat of nuclear destruction ended with the brief appearance and disappearance of Gorbachev.

Nuclear weapons are not under safe control within the vast spaces of the former Soviet Union. And the countries of the Middle East (not to mention, so we are told, North Korea) are feverishly purchasing American and other scientific know-how so as to enable them to make their own nuclear weapons, for what purposes imagination does not suffice.

The problems of our own time have two common denominators. The first and most elementary is that all of them, no matter how local they may appear on the surface, are global in their ultimate effects. None is purely domestic. None can be solved by one nation. How ironic it is that the triumphs of science and technology have made us in almost every arena except possibly health, and I am not sure even of that, not more secure but more vulnerable, and that the spectacular strides in wealth and power have made us not more secure but more fragile. The tremor of every earthquake, even in the most distant lands, is felt, as it were, in every American community. Contemplate our almost automatic response now to what happens in Iraq, in the former Yugoslavia, in Somalia, etc. That was not true fifty years ago or thirty years ago. So too with the news of almost every natural phenomenon. Whatever crisis or tyranny—the schistosomiasis in the Nile Valley, famine in Bangladesh, pollution in the Mediterranean, oil leaks off the Brittany coast and Nantucket and Alaska—all are associated with symbols, such as the symbol of the computer or the symbol of Dr. Strangelove; all introduce nightmares in their uncertainty. If these and scores of analogous problems are capable of solution, or even of control, they must be resolved or controlled by cooperation among nations. None can be resolved in the laboratory of one nation.

A second common denominator is that most of our contemporary problems—not, to be sure, those related to what I call "dementia"—can yield to the application of science and technology if wisely directed. The world does seem to command the skills with which to deal with most of them, with population or with eradication of many of the communicable diseases, or the dissipation of industrial pollution, or the elimination of atomic weapons. What we lack is not science or knowledge but boldness, resourcefulness, courage, and creativity. Only the smaller nations of the globe seem to display these qualities. Perhaps only they can afford to indulge in them.

There are special circumstances that make it difficult, to be sure, for Americans today to deal with their problems with any effectiveness. There is the paradox that just at a time when we are dazzled by discoveries in outer space, we have come to the end of the concept that has consoled us for two centuries, the notion of an infinity of resources, and we are forced now to accommodate as best we can to a nation and a world of finite resources. Our failure to cope with the energy crisis is, I think, sufficient testimony to the psychological shock of the situation. If we who have but six percent of the world's population, but consume forty percent of its resources, are unable to accommodate ourselves to this crisis, what reason is there to suppose that more numerous and vastly poorer peoples and nations can and will do so?

Another reason it is difficult for us to deal with problems is that we have finally reached the end of isolation in America, not just political or cultural isolation, but economic, technological, and scientific. Some may remember Beard's prescription for the crisis of the 1930s, what he called "continentalism": just withdraw into our own continent and let the rest of the world go hang; we could survive no matter what happened to the Old World. We assumed then that Americans were indeed in control, that they could take care of their own crises without outside aid. Some of our more Neanderthal politicians still seem to think it profitable to cater to this illusion, though no one seriously believes it anymore. Yet we still have not built that network of cooperative activities, pooling of knowledge and pooling of controls, more essential in the economic and ecological and scientific areas even than in the political. Though thoughtful people now recognize the interdependence of all nations and of all the resources of the globe, many of us still cling to the older assumptions of independence and self-sufficiency, and this both in the political realm and in the ecological. We are still prisoners of our familiar clichés, still imprisoned in our fears and suspicions and our pride and our talk. We have learned a good deal in the past three decades, to be sure. We may even have learned enough to abandon the notion that we are somehow an Asian power, and to realize that we cannot order the affairs of Africa, but we still try to intervene in the domestic affairs of a good many of the nations of the globe. We still think we can dispose of our own resources and the resources of the seas around us pretty much as we please. We still prefer unilateral action to international action. We still stick to ideas of the now departed Cold War, though not as convincingly as we did in the past, and to some of the tactics and strategy as well. Indeed, though we have abandoned most of the more aggressive policies we adopted in the 1950s and 1960s and have conceded the error, if not the moral culpability, of our intervention in Southeast Asia, we have not yet wholly repudiated the assumptions on which those policies were based. We still assume, too, that God and nature require that the United States be number one in almost everything, certainly in arms. (A nation, I might note parenthetically, that interprets being number one in military terms is like a university that interprets being number one in terms of football prowess.)

The society requires to be rebuilt, wrote John Stuart Mill over a century ago; "There is no use attempting to rebuild on the old plan. No great improvements in the lot of man are possible until a great change takes place in the fundamental constitution of our modes of thought." A revolution in our modes of thought should not be as difficult for Americans as for most other peoples. Certainly, we were able to achieve such a revolution in the past far more easily than other nations. Our revolutions have not on the whole been violent, but legal and even respectable. But of late we have become like other and older peoples, more set in our ways, reluctant to innovate and almost impotent to create except in the realm of science. Ours is not elsewhere a creative age. It is certainly not a creative age in the realm of politics. There it is almost shockingly unimaginative. What is called for if we are to survive is a radical reconstruction of our political and, I believe, our philosophical thinking, certainly of our moral attitudes.

On the philosophical agenda must be a recognition of the interdependence of all peoples and nations. This in turn will call for a radical rethinking of the nature of traditional nationalism. Nationalism is no doubt the most powerful force in modern history, perhaps because it has been chronologically associated with the industrial revolution and the modern scientific revolution. So bemused are we by this fact that we are sometimes tempted to believe that nationalism is somehow part of the cosmic system, but it is in fact a very recent phenomenon. Modern nationalism dates from the American and the French revolutions. It has lasted a far shorter time than the Roman Empire, a far shorter time than feudalism. It may disappear as those ultimately disappeared, though with a bang rather than with a whimper.

We are now in the midst of a dual revolution with respect to nationalism, one part quantitatively new and the other qualitatively very, very old. What is new is the burgeoning of nationalism throughout the globe. When the United Nations was formed, nearly fifty years ago, it numbered a total of some 50 nations. Now that number is 159. What is old is the widespread association of nationalism with ideology; that is the form which nationalism took in the sixteenth and seventeenth centuries, when it was largely an instrument of religion, though it was sometimes the other way around. Most Western nations drifted away from their ideological foundations, but what we now see in many parts of the globe is a revived and quickened and exacerbated association of nationalism with ideology, notably religious, as in the Middle East and on the subcontinent of India.

History teaches us that nothing is more dangerously explosive than the association of nationalism with ideology, yet this is what the former Soviet Union and the other parts of the communist globe consistently encouraged and financed, and it is what the capitalist United States, unconsciously perhaps, has consistently fomented and financed. That is the underlying explanation of the prolonged war in Vietnam, where three great powers—but only the United States openly—fought out their ideological differences in Vietnam, Laos, and Cambodia. That too is a partial explanation of our continuous intervention in Latin America. Perhaps we have reached a turning point now with the ratification of the Panama treaty, which may make it far easier to abandon some of the earlier consequences of American imperialism. Yet since World War II, we have had frequent examples of intervention in Latin America—in

Guatemala, Cuba, the Dominican Republic, Brazil, Chile, Panama. That policy threatened to embroil us in the internecine wars of Africa, where, fortunately, thanks rather to the Congress than to the State Department, we were turned back from getting mired in the morass.

Africa provides us with a sobering example of the dangers implicit in the national and ideological approach to the problems that threaten mankind. Civil wars, terrorism, struggles between rival armies and military contingents from other continents, all of these are directed, so it seems, to political, military, and ideological supremacy. Great nations like the United States, the former Soviet Union, and China have allowed themselves to be drawn into this vortex. Yet few of these conflicts touched the real problems of Africa, which could not be settled by arms—no matter who won, Africa would lose—and could not even be settled by politics.

The real problems of Africa were, as they are today, at once more elementary and more intractable. It still has the fastest growing population of any continent on the globe and the most rapidly exhausting resources of any continent on the globe. The Sahara desert is advancing sixty miles every year onto arable cropland and forests. It is a continent shattered by disease and malnutrition, spreading more rapidly and taking a heavier toll than on any other continent. It is a continent given over to illiteracy and to hatreds, racial and tribal. These problems simply cannot be solved by arms or by politics, nor by making demands on the African economy for oil or for other export commodities to help pay for imported arms or support footloose local politicians. If these problems are to be solved, it must be by science, medicine, and technology; by programs to limit the birthrate; by a restoration of the ecological balance, which has been hopelessly disrupted by the claims of industrialization and the exhaustion of natural resources. If the great powers were prepared to spend on these programs one percent of what they spent or induced the Africans to spend on the military, the tensions that are steadily driving the continent to self-destruction might be abated.

The crisis of Africa, which can be paralleled in the Caribbean and parts of Central and South America and much of Asia, dramatizes the need for transforming our modes of thought, a revolution in our concept of national security. That phrase, a phrase which has been invoked incessantly in our political discussions, is almost always interpreted in military terms. That is not only a narrow and vulgar concept, but a disastrous one. True national security is to be found, as Francis Bacon observed three centuries ago, not in armaments or war, but in the hearts and the minds of the people. It is to be found in their health, their intelligence and resourcefulness, their courage, their integrity. History, so men believed for many, many centuries, is philosophy teaching by example. If that is true, surely we have enough examples to make clear the nature of security, these from the calamitous Sicilian expedition of the Athenians that Thucydides chronicled for us, down to the arrogance and corruption of Hitler's Nazi regime, which led to the destruction of much of Europe. Security is to be found not only in the human but also in the natural resources of a people, the preservation of their soil and of their forests, their waters, their resources of oil and coal and gas and metals. It is to be found in respect for and in working with the balance of nature, nature which has nothing to do with the artificialities of nationalism. Might it not indeed be said that the very term *national security* is an oxymoron, for the globe is a seamless web of nature. Just as whatever threatens any part, however minute, of the human body threatens the health and the life of the individual, so whatever threatens nature in any part of the globe threatens security everywhere. The pollution of the seas not only kills species of fish, thus dangerously reducing food supplies of many peoples, but in the process upsets that delicate balance of nature developed over millions of years in the waters and the oceans. Erosion of the soil, substituting deserts for forests or for arable land, has repercussions throughout every continent. The purely military interpretation of national security with which we now bemuse ourselves may in fact be the most dangerous of all threats to our security. It makes intolerable claims on those natural resources that belong to posterity, and it distorts the economy, makes pernicious demands on the energies and talents of the people, invades the sanctity of the academy, distracts science from its proper occupations, foments secrecy in politics and public affairs, threatens the integrity of the constitutional political system, and tempts even a moral people to acts of gross immorality.

Consideration of the overwhelming importance of natural resources to national and international security leads us inevitably to an area that invites, if it does not indeed require, a revolution in our thinking, namely, our assumptions about public and private enterprise, or, to put the matter in Tocquevillian terms, about the relations of equality, on the one hand, and individualism, on the other. Already the line between public and private enterprise is blurred. The notion that there is a difference between a public university and a private university, between what is taught at the University of Chicago or what is taught at Indiana University, is of course absurd. Scholars are the same at both places, students the same, the apparatus of the laboratory and the library is the same; no scholar teaches Shakespeare differently at Chicago or Indiana or conducts experiments differently. We all accept that as a matter of fact in this all-important academic and scientific arena, and yet we somehow delude ourselves that in the economic arena and others there is a profound difference between public and private enterprise. That line, already blurred, may eventually be erased. An even partial solution to the problems of energy and natural resources, of unemployment, of the control of pollution, etc., will almost inevitably require a radical reconsideration of our habits and attitudes of ownership, and control and regulation, of natural resources. Of the two, by the way, it is probably the administration and regulation rather than the ownership that is ultimately important. It is a serious question whether mankind can much longer afford to leave the exploitation of the oil, the minerals, the forests, the waters, and the oceans to the vagaries of private enterprise. Certainly, it can be argued that all natural resources belong to the nation that in turn must dispose of them as best serves not just the immediate but also the long-term interests of the entire people, and the words *entire people* may come to mean more than the people of just one nation.

This crucial question was very much in the mind of Alexander Hamilton, then and since the patron saint of what is called "conservatism." Writing in the last number of the *Federalist Papers*, he stated,

> Mines in every country constitute a branch of revenue. In this country where nature has so richly impregnated the bowels of the earth they may in time become a very valuable one, and as they require the care and attention of government to protect, bring them to perfection, this care and a share in the profits of it should properly devolve upon Congress. All the precious metals should absolutely be the property of the federal government, and with respect to the others it should have the discretionary power of reserving the nature of a tax such part

as it may judge not inconsistent with the encouragement of so important an object.

The time may come, and in the not distant future, when nations will be forced to cooperate to preserve the natural resources of the earth for all mankind and for posterity. We may indulge ourselves and take for granted that the people of Africa or of Asia will quietly starve to death rather than challenge the use or misuse of resources by great powers, but how long would we take for granted that the nations of the Middle East could deny us access to their oil without intervention on our part? Indeed, when there was a threat, the Desert War began. We may take for granted that the wealth of the seas belongs to those fortunate nations with long coast lines. We would not take the same position if we were landlocked. Jefferson, by the way, toyed with the idea, as he toyed with all scientific ideas, of deflecting the Gulf Stream to warm the waters and the lands of New England and the Maritime Provinces of Canada, rather than letting all that warmth go off to the Old World. Would we permit Peru to deflect the waters of the Japan Current, the Humboldt Current? Would Northern Europe permit us today to deflect the Gulf Stream, if that could be done? As we are already moving toward a new and elaborate law of the seas, which will realize in more realistic fashion the necessity of international controls, so we must prepare for a much larger body of international law to preserve the resources of the land, the air, and outer space from national or ideological control.

What is at stake here, too, we should keep in mind, is not just what may be conceived of as the national interest of our generation; what is at stake is the interest and welfare of posterity, a posterity which may still be around long after the organization of the globe into national units may be as remote as feudalism is to us today. That extraordinary and farsighted novelist and scientist H. G. Wells saw this with characteristic prescience many years ago. "It is manifest," he wrote, "that unless some unity of purpose can be reached in the world, unless the ever more violent and disastrous incidents of war can be averted, unless some common control can be imposed on the headlong waste of man's limited inheritance of coal, oil, and moral energy than is now going on, the history of humanity itself must presently culminate in disaster."

As John Stuart Mill observed, institutional changes cannot be expected to work unless a company is inspired by moral and philosophical changes. Such changes are not to be brought about by moral preachments. They come, if they do come, from experience. Have we, as a people or as a government, learned anything from the long series of defeats and disasters of the past half century? Have we learned that we are not the peculiar agents of God or nature to impose order on a disorderly world, that we are no more an Asian power than China is an American power, that we cannot have our way in Africa, the Middle East, or on the great subcontinent of India and Pakistan? We have learned some things in the international arena; we have learned enough to withdraw from ownership and control of the Panama Canal, but not learned enough to have proposed what seems to me the most imaginative and effective of all solutions, handing over the canal jointly with Panama to the United Nations for their administration and control, as all comparable things should be under international administration to withdraw them from the vagaries and the dangers of war. Have we learned in the international arena to abide by the first great categorical imperative of Immanuel Kant, that we treat every nation and people as ends in themselves, not as means to our ends? Have we taken to heart the implications of the second great Kantian imperative, that we should so conduct ourselves as a nation that our every act can be generalized into a universal moral law?

There is no easy formula for restoration and reformation. What is required is that those changes in our philosophical attitudes that Mill called for should be easier for us than for most peoples of the Old World or Third World to embrace, for they constitute in reality but a return to what was long familiar in our history, even if it has been forgotten for the last century. This was a creed of the Founding Fathers that America had a moral responsibility to the whole of mankind. That creed flourished well into the nineteenth century. It received a religious and philosophical formulation at the hands of transcendentalists. After Emerson and the others it lingered on into the era of the post–Civil War years, what Vernon L. Parrington called "the great barbecue." Listen to the aged Emerson, speaking on the fortune of the Republic. "Power can be generous," he said, explaining that

> the very grandeur of the means which offer themselves to us should suggest grandeur in the direction of our expenditures. If our mechanic arts are unsurpassed in usefulness, if we have taught the river to make shoes and nails and carpets, and the bolt from heaven to write our letters, let these wonders work for honest humanity, for the poor, for justice, for genius, and for the public good. Let us realize that this country, the last found, is the great charity of God to the human race.

And in the same address he said, "I wish to see America, not like the old powers of the earth, grasping, exclusive, and narrow, but a benefactor such as no country ever was, hospitable to all nations, legislating for all nationalities. Nations were made to help each other as much as families were and all advancement is by ideas, not by brute force or mechanic force. Morality," he concluded, "is the object of government."

What is called for, then, is not a radical departure from our own traditions, but a return to those traditions. To achieve this calls for a revival of true conservatism. That conservatism must be distinguished both from the conservatism of the Old World, which we associate with Burke, Chateaubriand, Burckhardt, and others, and from the pseudoconservatives of our own time. The earlier conservatism, the European, is really totally alien to us. The Burkian conservatism rested on three stout pillars—the pillar of the monarchy, the pillar of the established church, and the pillar of centuries and centuries of history. We do not have a monarchy, and we do not have an established church. We do not have Europe's history. If we are to develop conservatism we have to develop our own kind. We cannot draw on Europe, something so many so-called intellectuals sometimes overlook. They are always going back to Burke or Burckhardt and thinking we can build on that. (Political conservatism today is, of course, a contradiction in terms, as it on the whole rather merits the term *anarchism* than *conservatism*.) American conservatism has its own foundations and its own history, its own logic, because, as Tocqueville pointed out, the American experience would come to mean more and more to emerging societies. The American conservatism is one that should prove acceptable to the Third World.

What is the true American conservatism? It is a philosophy that conserves the essential things—nature, man, and history or civilization. The prudent conservation of the whole of nature's gifts to man, or God's gifts, is of course the basic conservative principle. That is why, among other reasons, our great conservatives have been Jefferson, Theodore Roosevelt, and Franklin Roosevelt, who devoted themselves more to this task than any other leaders in our society have done.

Another element of conservatism is conservation of man himself, his physical well-being, his talents, his dignity as a human being, the opportunity to use and not waste all those resources and talents that he might have, just as embodied in the phrase, "life, liberty, and the pursuit of happiness." Again, it is Jefferson who is the symbol of this, Jefferson who wanted equality for all men, even for blacks, though he could not achieve it. This aspect of American conservatism has a long series of climactic moments: the opening of the public domain, which enabled ordinary men and women to become independent; the making of education available to all, common education and eventually higher education; the long and checkered crusade for equality for blacks, something we have not yet fully achieved. For reasons rooted in our long history of individualism and private enterprise, the United States came late to the welfare state, but with that greatest of modern conservatives, Franklin Roosevelt, we achieved something like true conservatism there in the conservation of the dignity and the welfare of men.

There is a conservatism of history and of traditions exemplified particularly by an awareness of our membership and our obligation to the much larger community of civilization. This is a concept that has deep roots in religion and deep roots, too, in that philosophy which prevailed at the time of the creation of the Republic, the Enlightenment. Historically, we may regard nationalism as a radical departure from these deeper conservatisms, a radical departure from the conservatism of the great community of faith and humanity, of science and art, which obtained not only in the Middle Ages, but in the era of the Enlightenment as well. Historically, it is nationalism that most drastically disrupted that community. We should take satisfaction here in our country in the reflection that while nationalism in the Old World—and generally, in the nineteenth and twentieth centuries, around the globe—had been a revolt against the great community, that was not the case of the emergence of nationalism in America in the eighteenth century. It is sufficient to recall that the very Declaration of Independence that announced to the world our nationalism appealed to the laws of nature and nature's God, acknowledged a decent respect for the opinions of mankind, set forth rights and principles that were the possession of all mankind. Need I add that every great American leader, from Washington and Jefferson to Lincoln to Woodrow Wilson and Franklin Roosevelt, acknowledged a responsibility of our membership in the great community of civilization? That responsibility can best be fulfilled by drawing on our own experience and invoking our own authority to solve national problems and applying the lessons of that experience to the challenges of the future.

Big government in the United States and elsewhere was not the product of ambition or aggrandizement, but of necessity, and indeed government itself was a product of necessity. Potentially in a Nazi, a fascist, a socialist state, big government is an instrument of tyranny, but the growth of national authority in our country has not been an instrument of tyranny, though with the growth of the military it could have become so. After all, it is the national government that has been the chief instrument of freedom, of democracy, and of prosperity in the United States. It put an end to slavery, emancipated women, set higher standards for equality in education, protected the rights of individuals and of minorities against local tyranny, established and broadened religious freedom. It did all of these things, not because its statesmen were wiser or more liberal than the statesmen who conducted state and local governments, but because the national government alone had both the power and the ability to act in these areas with any degree of effectiveness. In the American past, what seemed to be local problems proved to be national, and to be manageable only when dealt with on a national scale.

So today and in the future national problems are really global, and they must be dealt with on a global scale. As reluctantly and grudgingly as Americans came to concede to their national government authority to deal with the problems that their state governments could not solve, so however reluctant we may be—not just we of America, but we of all nations—we must concede to international regulatory commissions authority to deal with problems that nations individually cannot solve. This is to be achieved, if it can be achieved, not by some abstract thing called "world government," but by international agreements enforced by member nations themselves, such as even now flourish in so many areas—international agencies and regulatory commissions to deal with epidemics, to formulate a law of the sea, to deal with problems of nourishment and agriculture or with plant and animal diseases, or with slavery where it appears on the globe, with these and a hundred other problems that no one nation can possibly solve and which unsolved will affect every nation.

In the past, it was the United States that provided both moral and practical leadership in a series of major revolutions. We took the lead in the creation of a nation out of colonies; we were the first people to make a nation, and the American Revolution marked the beginning of the end of colonialism on the globe. In organizing a national constitution and in placing government under law, we pioneered, as we pioneered in creating a federal system and making it work. We were the first people successfully to limit government, inventing in the process the effective separation of powers and judicial review. We inaugurated modern democratic government. We were the first Western nation to separate church and state and to make real religious freedom. We were the first to make possible effective social equality, among whites at least, though as far as the blacks are concerned we lag far behind.

Another task now awaits us. Young William Wetmore Story, the great sculptor who was also trained as a lawyer, wrote a biography of his father, the distinguished Justice Story, and he reminds us of the elder Story's last lecture at Harvard Law School, the institution he revitalized and which he dominated for so much of his life. He was speaking and he was carried away, says his son, "by his own eloquence. He reminded his students of the hopes for freedom with which America was freighted, the anxious eyes that watched its progress, the voices that called from land to land to enquire of its welfare." And he admonished them "to labor for the furtherance of justice and free principles and to seek in all their public acts to establish the foundations of right and truth." If we are to recover that moral and practical leadership which we exercised at the time of the Revolution and during part of the nineteenth century, and again in the crises of the first and second World Wars, we should seek once again to establish, in all our acts, this time for the world, foundations of right and truth. This requires that we recognize the unity of mankind, the unity of that fragile fabric of resources on whose existence the welfare of mankind depends, the unity of the human race, not only horizontally as it were, throughout the present-day world, but vertically as well, a unity that requires we address ourselves always to the interests of posterity.